Freedom of Speech in Universities

Freedom of speech and extremism in university campuses are major sources of debate and moral panic in the United Kingdom today. In 2018, the Joint Committee on Human Rights in Parliament undertook an inquiry into freedom of speech on campus. It found that much of the public concern is exaggerated, but identified a number of factors that require attention, including the impact of government counter-terrorism measures (the Prevent Duty) and regulatory bodies (including the Charity Commission for England and Wales) on freedom of speech.

This book combines empirical research and philosophical analysis to explore these issues, with a particular focus on the impact upon Muslim students and staff. It offers a new conceptual paradigm for thinking about freedom of speech, based on deliberative democracy, and practical suggestions for universities in handling it.

Topics covered include

- The enduring legacy of key thinkers who have shaped the debate about freedom of speech
- The role of right-wing populism in driving moral panic about universities
- The impact of the Prevent Duty and the Charity Commission upon Muslim students, students' unions and university managers
- Students' and staff views about freedom of speech
- Alternative approaches to handling freedom of speech on campus, including the Community of Inquiry

This highly engaging and topical text will be of interest to those working within public policy, religion and education or religion and politics and Islamic Studies.

Alison Scott-Baumann is Professor of Society and Belief at the School of Oriental and African Studies, UK.

Simon Perfect is a researcher and tutor at the School of Oriental and African Studies, UK.

Islam in the World

Freedom of Speech in Universities
Islam, Charities and Counter-terrorism
Alison Scott-Baumann and Simon Perfect

Freedom of Speech in Universities
Islam, Charities and Counter-terrorism

Alison Scott-Baumann and Simon Perfect

LONDON AND NEW YORK

First published 2021
by Routledge
2 Park Square, Milton Park, Abingdon, Oxon OX14 4RN

and by Routledge
52 Vanderbilt Avenue, New York, NY 10017

Routledge is an imprint of the Taylor & Francis Group, an informa business

© 2021 Alison Scott-Baumann and Simon Perfect

The right of Alison Scott-Baumann and Simon Perfect to be identified as authors of this work has been asserted by them in accordance with sections 77 and 78 of the Copyright, Designs and Patents Act 1988.

All rights reserved. No part of this book may be reprinted or reproduced or utilised in any form or by any electronic, mechanical, or other means, now known or hereafter invented, including photocopying and recording, or in any information storage or retrieval system, without permission in writing from the publishers.

Trademark notice: Product or corporate names may be trademarks or registered trademarks, and are used only for identification and explanation without intent to infringe.

British Library Cataloguing-in-Publication Data
A catalogue record for this book is available from the British Library

Library of Congress Cataloging-in-Publication Data
A catalog record has been requested for this book

ISBN: 978-0-367-25782-8 (hbk)
ISBN: 978-0-429-28983-5 (ebk)

Typeset in Times New Roman
by SPi Global, India

Contents

List of figures and table   vi
Acknowledgements   vii

   Introduction   1

1 Freedom of speech: understanding the ideas   12

2 Populism, freedom of speech and human rights   32

3 The Prevent Duty and the views of university Prevent Leads   48

4 External agitators and students' views about freedom of speech and Prevent   70

5 Charity law, political activism and speaking freely in students' unions   88

6 The Charity Commission's interventions in students' unions   102

7 Improving conversations about difficult topics   119

Appendix: Community of Inquiry (CofI)   133
Index   138

Figures and table

Figures

6.1 Full student sample knowledge of, and attitude towards, the Charity Commission's involvement in oversight of students' unions — 105

6.2 Muslim students' knowledge of, and attitude towards, the Charity Commission's involvement in oversight of students' unions — 106

Table

1.1 A fourfold model for handling freedom of speech — 27

Acknowledgements

We wish to thank Dr Katherine Brown and Professor Jorgen Nielsen, editors for the Routledge *Islam in the World* series, for commissioning this book and supporting us. Thank you also to Rebecca Shillabeer, publisher at Routledge, and Dr Amy Doffegnies, Editorial Assistant at Routledge, for enduring guidance, and to Dr David Perfect and Dr Jill Collens for their huge help with references and proofreading.

In addition we would like to thank the following for their invaluable contributions in various ways: Dr Tarek Al Baghal, Peter Baran, Chris Beal, Shahanaz Begum, Dr Rob Faure Walker, Dr Alec Hamilton, Professor John Holmwood, John Lotherington, Lottie Moore, Professor Chris Norris, Hasan Pandor and Dr Roy Sloan.

Most importantly, we wish to thank our families for their endless patience, encouragement and love: Mike, Lizzie, James, Benjie and Alice; Judith, Dave, Jill and Jonathan. We couldn't have done this without you.

Introduction

UK universities are in trouble. COVID-19 has swung a wrecking ball at their finances, and many face difficult decisions about how to balance the books. As of the summer 2020, the long-term losses to the Higher Education sector are predicted to be anywhere between £3 and 19 billion (Drayton and Waltmann, 2020: 2).

But the current disaster comes on top of a more fundamental crisis – a crisis of public confidence in universities and their apparent failure to be the bastions of liberal democracy that they are meant to be. Central to this are claims about freedom of speech, extremism and Muslims on campus. Rigorous, open debate is supposed to be at the core of university life, but students are regularly accused of being intolerant of people who express views they do not like and shutting down legitimate debate to avoid offending minority groups, or, conversely, of hosting people (usually Muslims) with 'extreme' views. A large proportion of the public shares these worries – a poll in 2019 found that 52% of British adults think that 'free speech is under threat' in UK universities (compared to only 14% who disagree), and nearly a third think that 'Islamic extremism' is common on campus (Perfect et al., 2019: 10).

Such moral concern about universities is not new. They have long been seen as hotbeds of left-wing radicalism, and in 1986, in response to student attempts on some campuses to disrupt visits by Conservative MPs, the government introduced the Education (No. 2) Act, which requires English and Welsh universities to uphold freedom of speech (Day and Dickinson, 2018: 34–36). For a while this appeared to settle the matter, but more recent governments have returned to treating universities as an important political issue. In 2015, the Conservatives introduced the Prevent Duty, the legal duty on universities (and other public institutions) to take steps to prevent people from being drawn into terrorism (the Counter-Terrorism and Security Act 2015).

They also empowered the Office for Students (OfS – the regulator for English universities from 2018) to sanction universities deemed to be failing to uphold freedom of speech (OfS, n.d.). Ministers have criticised a supposed campus culture of illiberal 'safetyism', with Jo Johnson (Minister for Universities and Science from 2015 to 2018) arguing that certain groups 'have sought to stifle those who do not agree with them in every way under the banner of "safe spaces" or "no-platforming"' (Johnson, 2017). In the current pandemic, the government has politicised the issue still further, saying that whether it bails out struggling universities will depend partly on how far they protect freedom of speech (Department for Education, 2020: 3–5).

But how fair are these concerns? In 2017–18, Parliament's Joint Committee on Human Rights (JCHR) conducted an inquiry into the issue and concluded that various factors may be chilling or stifling freedom of speech on campus. But it also argued that much of the public concern is overblown: 'The press accounts of widespread suppression of free speech are clearly out of kilter with reality' (JCHR, 2018: 19). Despite this important intervention, the public (and political) anxiety about universities persists.

The current debate hinges on a binary narrative: that on the one hand, universities and their students are unfairly restricting legitimate freedom of speech, and that on the other, they are giving *too much* freedom to extremists. These claims are often based more on anecdote and moral panic than on reliable evidence. They also focus primarily on, and blame, the activities of students, rather than interrogating wider structures on campus that shape the dynamics of freedom of speech. This book combines new empirical research and philosophical analysis to improve our understanding and help us move beyond these narratives. It pays particular attention to the experiences of Muslim students, staff and external speakers; what happens to them is an early warning sign of what will at some point affect all university members.

The focus of and need for this book

This book is for anyone interested in freedom of speech debates on campus – including journalists, policymakers and university staff and students – and anyone who wants to learn how better to handle difficult conversations on divisive topics. Our work aligns with current attempts to rejuvenate democracy: institutionalising citizens' deliberative processes of decision making within universities and creating ways of influencing government. We believe that freedom of speech is core to universities because uninhibited discussion is key for the learning process and for the production and dissemination of knowledge. Moreover, by championing this freedom and creating space for rigorous debate of important issues, universities play a critical role in maintaining democracy's vitality.

The book has two main goals, one specific and the other broad. The specific goal is to show that when thinking about freedom of speech in universities, we miss important pieces of the puzzle if we focus only on student actions. Instead, we need to pay attention to two important regulatory structures that shape freedom of speech on campus: first, the Prevent Duty, and second, charity law as it applies to students' unions and their regulation (in most cases) by the Charity Commission for England and Wales. These structures are particularly relevant for Muslims on campus, but also affect the learning experience of all students and staff. To explore this, we set out findings from our empirical research (conducted between 2015 and 2019) with university managers responsible for implementing the Prevent Duty, with students' union staff and with students themselves, including Muslims. We show how these two structures push students and staff to be risk-averse and even self-censorial. Some of the evidence we examine here was submitted to the JCHR's inquiry and played an important role in focusing the MPs' attention on these structural factors (JCHR, 2018: 34–37).

The broader goal is to help readers think about freedom of speech issues in a more balanced way than the binary we are usually presented with – where one either supports that freedom or wants to restrict it. We set out a new paradigm for thinking about different positions on freedom of speech – a model with four distinct approaches: libertarian, liberal, guarded liberal and no-platforming. We make practical recommendations for university staff and students about how to use this model for handling the tension between upholding freedom of speech and protecting vulnerable groups from harm. We offer a staff- and student-based approach to nurturing freedom of speech, in contrast to the top-down, compulsion-based approach used by the government.

Everyone should care about these issues, whether they are involved in Higher Education or not. Universities are the primary institutions that are able to – and indeed expected to – host debate about difficult topics, challenging the perceived orthodoxies of society. We should all be concerned if there are factors that chill freedom of speech in them.

These issues are particularly important right now. Far-right groups are stirring up hatred against Muslims and other minorities and in some cases committing acts of terrorism. Terrorism from ISIS and other jihadist groups remains a threat to the West, and right-wing populists have come to power on anti-Muslim platforms. In the United Kingdom, Remainers and Leavers continue to be deeply divided after the 2016 vote to leave the EU. At the time of writing, the COVID-19 pandemic is exacerbating existing inequalities between rich and poor (Blundell et al., 2020; Perfect, 2020). White supremacist groups have exploited the situation to recruit people to their causes. As people have stayed isolated at home and online, there has been an increased danger of online hate speech, online radicalisation and the spread of conspiracy theories (Commission for Countering Extremism, 2020; Institute for Strategic Dialogue, 2020).

All this is happening as the way we communicate is transformed. Social media companies wield immense power over how we express ourselves, our social and political choices, and even our knowledge about the world. These technologies encourage us to remain in echo chambers, talking only to those like us, except for moments of shouting opinions at strangers with no real listening. Often, what we say online *about* people and the degree of offence we experience or deliver have become the measure of our relationships, rather than the time we spend trying to communicate *with* each other civilly. The online world is also sexist: as Mary Beard, classicist and public intellectual, explains: 'a significant subsection is directed at silencing the woman' (Beard, 2017: 37). In this polarised, digital world, we need to learn how to debate well with people with very different views from ours, and how best to handle speech (online or offline) that we find grossly offensive or harmful.

We give especial attention in this book to Muslim members of universities. In part this is because the regulatory structures we consider have a disproportionate impact on Muslims' freedom to speak. It is also because Muslims are at the heart of debates about freedom of speech today and are regular targets of right-wing populists who claim for themselves the mantle of defenders of freedom of speech. The idea that Muslims and Islam oppose freedom of speech is a core Orientalist trope, long used by Western commentators to present the West, by contrast, as the realm of the free. Critics of Islam bolster this claim by pointing to restrictions on speech in authoritarian Muslim-majority countries, and also to cases of global protest, or even violence, by Muslims reacting to literature or images deemed blasphemous.

Yet Muslims today find themselves victimised by others who use their right to freedom of speech to express Islamophobic hate speech. Hate speech (of any kind) can exert a silencing effect on victims. In the COVID-19 pandemic, for example, there is evidence that racism experienced by some ethnic minority National Health Service workers made them reluctant to speak out about issues like personal protective equipment shortages, putting their lives at risk (Public Health England, 2020: 33). When people fear negative consequences, or think their views will not be considered valid, some decide not to speak out about injustices they face. We show how this affects Muslim students on campus.

It should be noted that while much of our analysis applies to all UK universities, some of our discussion focuses primarily on English and Welsh institutions, due to diversity in the relevant legal frameworks. Under the Human Rights Act 1998, universities across the United Kingdom are required to uphold Article 10, the right to freedom of expression (including the right to express views that may offend, shock or disturb others). They can only restrict this right in limited circumstances, for example, to prevent speakers from infringing the rights of others (Human Rights Act 1998, s. 6) (Equality and Human Rights Commission [EHRC], 2019: 8–12). But English and Welsh universities have an additional legal duty to have a free speech code of practice, and to take 'reasonably practicable' steps to secure freedom of speech within the law for staff, students and visiting speakers. This includes ensuring, 'so far as is reasonably practicable', that use of premises (including students' union premises) is not denied to anyone on account of their beliefs (Education (No. 2) Act 1986, s. 43). Meanwhile, our discussion of the Prevent Duty is relevant for England, Wales and Scotland but not for Northern Ireland (which has no such duty), and in Chapters 5 and 6 our focus is on students' unions regulated by the Charity Commission for England and Wales.[1]

Finally, a word on terminology. Much of our discussion refers to concepts like 'extremism', 'radicalisation' and 'hate speech'. We do not define them, precisely because they are highly contested, politicised concepts. We show that their use often leads to confusion and exaggeration. We recommend a critical approach to such terms in order to increase the possibility of honest and open debate.

Is speech a right, a risk or a reciprocity?

Debates about freedom of speech are often impoverished because they are rooted only in legal and empirical analysis, or only in philosophical reflection. This book brings the two approaches together. It is essential that those interested in handling freedom of speech practically (including university managers and policymakers) get a better understanding of the conceptual issues underpinning it.

There are two contrasting trends in contemporary discussions about freedom of speech: feeling entitled to freedom of speech as an absolute right, and feeling fearful of freedom of speech because it can create risk. These map on to the binary narrative of moral panic about universities.

The first trend is a tendency to see the exercise of speech solely as a matter of *rights*, leading people to view their own right to speak as paramount and unqualified. Such libertarian discourse does not take into account how the exercise of one's rights directly affects (or impedes) other people's rights. At the extremes, we see this among people devoted to noninterventionism with a neoliberal flavour, who advocate full freedom to market forces, and believe that government intervention (and sometimes even human rights legislation itself) is counterproductive to individual liberty. Underpinning this is an assumption that all ideas, no matter how offensive, should be fully free to circulate in a 'marketplace of ideas'. In the university context, it leads to condemnation of any attempt to limit freedom of speech as morally bankrupt, regardless of its motivation.

This tendency fails to recognise the limitations of rights-based arguments within a liberal democracy. Human rights discourse seeks to protect everyone's safety and dignity equally; it positions rights as universal and immutable. This has not, of course, gone unchallenged historically; the utilitarian philosopher Jeremy Bentham (1748–1832) ridiculed the idea that any human has rights, including a natural entitlement to personal protection, as 'nonsense upon stilts' (Schofield et al., 2002). Today such criticisms are rare. But contemporary scholars like Heinze (2016) and Rivers (2018) show that liberal democracies depend upon theoretical structures built upon rights that they can neither implement nor fully control. In a liberal democracy, different individuals' rights must be balanced against each other, and not everyone's rights (including the right to freedom of speech) can be exercised fully. In practice, such countries protect the rights of some at the cost of others. Additionally, we find the rights discourse (particularly the appeal to freedom of speech rights) being hijacked by people with power to cement their own position over more vulnerable groups.

The second trend, conversely, is a tendency to view freedom of speech primarily through the lens of managing *risk*. Out of fear of causing offence, people often self-censor their views. While this is normal to maintain the harmony of everyday relationships, there is a danger the concern about the risk of causing offence can lead to people avoiding important, though controversial, conversations – or further, preventing others from engaging in them. On campus, this trend manifests itself as an aversion to voices or topics that may offend minority groups, prioritising protecting those groups from potential offence over unrestricted freedom of speech. Taken to extremes, it can lead to the silencing of particular voices or topics (which, as explained in Chapter 1, we call no-platforming).

Yet some people speak less freely not because they are concerned about offending people, and more because they worry they will be viewed as a security threat. This is a particular issue among Muslims. It encourages risk aversion, which at worst motivates people to avoid voicing any opinion that differs from that of the majority. In turn, our shared public understanding is impoverished. It also creates a democratic deficit, whereby citizens are ignorant of aspects of their relationship with the state, and the government sees no need to enlighten them. We will show how this plays out on campus.

The UK government's counter-terrorism policy is also shaped by the tendency to see freedom of speech as a (security) risk to be managed. In the university context, this manifests in attempts to restrict speech of people with controversial or extreme views. Such policies find particularly vocal support from neoconservative voices, who support tough security measures against the threat of terrorism, including restrictions on certain people's speech. In Higher Education, these neoconservative voices are a counterweight to the neoliberal advocacy of nonintervention and unqualified freedom of speech.

These two trends drive much of the tension about freedom of speech in universities. The two extremes can cancel each other out and make it impossible to move forward. Amy Fenton, a journalist for *The Mail*, a newspaper in Barrow, Northern England, learnt this when she complained to the police about the threats of violence she received for reporting on complex legal cases: 'the consistent message I got from the police when I reported it was that they had to balance these individuals' right to freedom of speech and expression with my right to be safe' (Pidd, 2020). The police felt unable to act for either party, showing the cancelling-out effect achieved by the binary of rights versus risks. Police inability to balance counterclaims only changed when Fenton's life was threatened.

Instead of risk aversion, we advocate *risk awareness*. This means taking seriously the need to uphold the right to freedom of speech for all, including for those with controversial views. At the same time, it means acknowledging the risk that in exercising this right, we might offend or hurt others, and then making a judgement about how best to respond. Risk awareness involves understanding both rights and risks. We feel entitled to put our view forward, and we know there is a risk attached – not least because we will have to challenge those who seek to shut us down, as well as accepting that we may be proved wrong. We show how to reduce the rights and risks complications.

Reciprocity is the key. Instead of viewing freedom of speech either as an absolute right (which can lead to a disregard for other people's rights) or only through the lens of risk management (which can lead to risk aversion), we see it as something requiring reciprocity, which involves discussions, or even arguments. As French philosopher Paul Ricoeur explained: 'Rights cannot be claimed on my behalf unless they are recognised in the same way for others' (Ricoeur, 2016: 293). Instead of the monologic outcome of speaking freely without considering how the exercise of my right affects others, or the silence that comes from risk aversion, we must communicate reciprocally, where everyone involved in a conversation acknowledges they have *obligations* to everyone else. These include an obligation to be explicit and open with the other, whose views must be recognised, however unpleasant they seem. Above all, this must take place as part of a conversation in which all parties share the right of reply and share the risk involved in trying to communicate well with each other. We must believe in the power of conversation to strengthen social bonds that bind us together and must work constantly to reinforce them.

Cultivating a culture of reciprocity can help us navigate our digital world. Online communication is open to manipulation: we are exposed to the rise of fake news, conspiracy theories, climate change deniers and other confusing, destructive phenomena. In response, it is very important consciously to develop our own moral framework so we become aware of our obligations to each other when speaking, online and offline; this will motivate us to communicate accurately, compassionately and responsibly. We need to have the confidence and competence to explain ourselves clearly and to challenge others to explain themselves. Being clear about the parameters of speech provides a way to avoid violence, to be conciliatory and to make oneself understood.

Perhaps most important of all, in order to take control of the way we share our thoughts, hopes and fears with others, we need confidence to debate important ideas. This is especially important in universities. Drawing on the ideas of American pragmatist thinker Charles Sanders Peirce (1839–1914), we show how universities can do this by developing a 'Community of Inquiry' (CofI – like 'coffee'). It is key for building a culture of reciprocity and for helping students and staff to speak freely in a risk-aware, not risk-averse, way. This is essential if universities are to respond to the structural pressures currently driving the free speech wars on campus and the wider pressures on citizens in society. Students are citizens and, as Chwalisz (2017) asserts, 'the public is a resource to be tapped, not a risk to be managed'.

Introduction 9

Overview of the book

Chapter 1 frames our discussion by examining key thinkers who have shaped the debate about freedom of speech, both historically and in modern times. We introduce our new paradigm for handling freedom of speech practically on campus.

Chapter 2 considers connections between populist politics, freedom of speech debates and Muslims. Grasping this context is key for understanding campus free speech wars because universities and students have become a staple target for right-wing populist discourse.

Chapter 3 analyses the development and operation of the Prevent Duty in universities since 2015. We consider its focus on Muslims and show how government guidance for the Duty encourages universities to be risk-averse. We also present findings from our research with 'Prevent Leads' – university managers with responsibility for the Duty – and examine their perceptions of it.

Chapter 4 explores how students see themselves and how influential external organisations see them. It analyses how the Henry Jackson Society, a neoconservative think tank, and *Spiked*, a libertarian magazine, shape public narratives about universities. It contrasts their views with data from surveys of student opinion about freedom of speech. Finally, it sets out findings from *Re/presenting Islam on Campus*, a major AHRC-funded research project (2015–18), showing the views of Muslim and non-Muslim students about Islam and Prevent.

Chapter 5 uncovers the impact of charity law on freedom of speech and political activism within students' unions since 2010. This key issue has received little prior attention. We draw on our research with students' union staff to show how charitable status has further pushed some students' unions towards risk aversion, with a disproportionate impact on Muslim students.

Chapter 6 follows on from the previous chapter by examining the impact of the Charity Commission for England and Wales. This regulates most UK students' unions. Through a detailed case study, we see how the Commission's intervention discourages unions from hosting controversial speakers.

Chapter 7 shows how universities can resist the impact of regulatory structures chilling freedom of speech, and how they can facilitate freer debate on campus. It explains the concept of Community of Inquiry and how this can be used alongside our new fourfold model of freedom of speech.

The Appendix provides a worked example of a Community of Inquiry, showing what this looks like in practice.

Notes

1 Other relevant laws include the duty (applicable across the United Kingdom) on universities to uphold academic freedom, including academics' right to put forward 'controversial or unpopular opinions' (Education Reform Act 1988, s. 202(2)(a); The Education (Academic Tenure) (Northern Ireland) Order, 1988, s. 3(2)(a)). Universities in England, Wales and Scotland must also comply with the Public Sector Equality Duty, meaning that, among other things, they need to consider the need to advance good relations between people who share a protected characteristic (such as a particular religion or belief) and people who do not. When making decisions about upholding freedom of speech, universities need to (at least) consider the potential impact on students who may feel vilified because of, for example, their religious identity (Equality Act 2010, s. 149; EHRC, 2019: 26). Students' unions are separate entities from their parent universities, so the legal duties to uphold freedom of speech and to prevent terrorism do not apply directly to them, though they affect them indirectly (EHRC, 2019: 15; 25).

References

Beard, M. (2017) *Women & Power: A Manifesto*. London: Profile Books Ltd.

Blundell, R., Joyce, M., Costa Dias, M., and Xu, X. (2020) *Covid-19: the Impacts of the Pandemic on Inequality*. IFS Briefing Note, 11 June. London: Institute for Fiscal Studies. https://www.ifs.org.uk/publications/14879.

Chwalisz, C. (2017) 'The People's Verdict: Adding Informed Citizen Voices to Public Decision-Making', *Policy Network*, 20 June. https://policynetwork.org/publications/books/the-peoples-verdict/.

Commission for Countering Extremism (2020) *COVID-19: How Hateful Extremists Are Exploiting the Pandemic*. London: Commission for Countering Extremism. https://assets.publishing.service.gov.uk/government/uploads/system/uploads/attachment_data/file/898925/CCE_Briefing_Note_001.pdf.

Day, M., and Dickinson, J. (2018) *David versus Goliath: The Past, Present and Future of Students' Unions in the UK*. HEPI Report No. 111. London: Higher Education Policy Institute. https://www.hepi.ac.uk/wp-content/uploads/2018/09/HEPI-Students-Unions-Report-111-FINAL-EMBARGOED1.pdf.

Department for Education (2020) *Establishment of a Higher Education Restructuring Regime in Response to COVID-19*. London: Department for Education. https://assets.publishing.service.gov.uk/government/uploads/system/uploads/attachment_data/file/902608/HERR_announcement_July_2020.pdf.

Drayton, E., and Waltmann, B. (2020) *Will Universities Need a Bailout to Survive the COVID-19 Crisis?* IFS Briefing Note BN300. London: Institute for Fiscal Studies. https://www.ifs.org.uk/uploads/BN300-Will-universities-need-bailout-survive-COVID-19-crisis-1.pdf.

Education (No. 2) Act (1986) https://www.legislation.gov.uk/ukpga/1986/61.

Equality and Human Rights Commission (EHRC) (2019) *Freedom of Expression in England and Wales; A Guide for Higher Education Providers and Students' Unions in England and Wales*. https://www.equalityhumanrights.com/sites/default/files/freedom-of-expression-guide-for-higher-education-providers-and-students-unions-england-and-wales.pdf.

Heinze, E. (2016) *Hate Speech and Democratic Citizenship*. Oxford: Oxford University Press.

Institute for Strategic Dialogue (2020) *COVID-19 Disinformation Briefing No. 1*. 27 March. London: Institute for Strategic Dialogue. https://www.isdglobal.org/wp-content/uploads/2020/06/COVID-19-Briefing-01-Institute-for-Strategic-Dialogue-27th-March-2020.pdf.

Johnson, J. (2017) '*Free Speech in the Liberal University*'. *Speech at the Limmud Conference*, Birmingham, 26 December. https://www.gov.uk/government/speeches/free-speech-in-the-liberal-university.

Joint Committee on Human Rights (JCHR) (2018) *Freedom of Speech in Universities*. House of Lords/House of Commons (HC 589; HL Paper 111): Fourth Report of Session 2017–19. London: The Stationery Office. https://publications.parliament.uk/pa/jt201719/jtselect/jtrights/589/589.pdf.

Office for Students (OfS) (n.d.) 'Freedom of Speech'. https://officeforstudents.org.uk/advice-and-guidance/student-wellbeing-and-protection/freedom-of-speech/what-can-we-do/

Perfect, S. (2020) *Bridging the Gap: Economic Inequality and Church Responses in the UK*. London: Theos. https://www.theosthinktank.co.uk/cmsfiles/Reportfiles/Theos---Bridging-the-Gap---Economic-Inequality-and-the-Churches.pdf.

Perfect, S., Aune, K., and Ryan, B. (2019) *Faith and Belief on Campus: Division and Cohesion. Exploring Student Faith and Belief Societies*. London: Theos. https://www.theosthinktank.co.uk/cmsfiles/Reportfiles/Theos---Faith-and-Belief-on-Campus---Division-and-Cohesion.pdf.

Pidd, H. (2020) 'Barrow Journalist Hounded out of Cumbria for Reporting Court Case', *The Guardian*, 29 May. https://www.theguardian.com/uk-news/2020/may/29/barrow-journalist-hounded-out-of-cumbria-for-reporting-court-case.

Public Health England (2020) *Beyond the Data: Understanding the Impact of COVID-19 on BAME Groups*. London: Public Health England. https://assets.publishing.service.gov.uk/government/uploads/system/uploads/attachment_data/file/892376/COVID_stakeholder_engagement_synthesis_beyond_the_data.pdf.

Ricoeur, P. (2016) *Philosophical Anthropology*. Cambridge: Polity.

Rivers, J. (2018) 'Counter-Extremism, Fundamental Values and the Betrayal of Liberal Democratic Constitutionalism', *German Law Journal*, 2: 267–299.

Schofield, P., Pease-Watkins, C. and Blamires, C. (eds.) (2002) *The Collected Works of Jeremy Bentham: Rights, Representation, and Reform: Nonsense upon Stilts and Other Writings on the French Revolution*. Oxford: Clarendon Press.

1 Freedom of speech
Understanding the ideas

Too often, we tend to see freedom of speech as a binary – you either support more of it or want to restrict it. This simplistic view obscures centuries of intellectual debate about what it means to speak freely, why it is important and where the boundaries of speech should lie. We cannot hope to change the polarised state of debate about speech today if we do not grapple with the ideas of key theorists.

This chapter begins with a brief consideration of thinking about freedom of speech in religious traditions, including Islam. It examines the ideas of key thinkers who have driven the intellectual debate about this freedom. Finally, it offers a new paradigm for thinking about how to handle freedom of speech practically, in universities and elsewhere. This fourfold model is summarised in Table 1.1.

The state, religions and the risks of freedom of speech

Debates about freedom of speech appear right at the beginning of Western philosophy. As the 'grandfather' of freedom of speech, Socrates believed that *parrhesia*, 'free speech', is a privilege with immense value. Through speaking freely, one ends up revealing one's own ignorance to oneself and to others and, most importantly, learns from that experience. Yet Plato, Socrates' pupil, saw freedom of speech as a potential risk – and as particularly dangerous when women speak (Beard, 2017: 3–43). Plato feared that in a fully democratic society, unrestricted speech could lead to ordinary people challenging the existing order and thus fracturing the state. This worry that freedom of speech can challenge a state is a recurrent theme in philosophy. It re-emerges today in government concern about 'extreme' speech on campus, which focuses upon religion, especially Islam.

Religious traditions have much to say about freedom of speech, as something that is both risky and to be defended. It is important to take account of historical religious thought here: today religions are often accused of wanting to curtail freedom of speech, which is imagined as a purely 'secular' principle. These are gross generalisations. In reality, the principles or rights seen as core to democracy in the West today (including religious liberty, freedom of speech and the concept of secularism itself) have roots in religious as well as freethinking ideas and historically were advocated by committed religious people as well as freethinkers, often against the religious and temporal authorities of their day. After the Second World War, moreover, Christian-inspired politicians in Europe were responsible for promoting the discourse of human rights, drawing on language like the dignity of the human 'person' which had origins in Catholic Social Teaching (Spencer, 2016: 134).[1]

That said, the limitations on freedom of speech within religious traditions should not be downplayed because they remain with us despite increasing secularisation. Many religions contain prohibitions against blasphemy – verbal or written expressions that attack religious tenets or structures that expert religious authorities view as orthodox. Many traditions regard such expressions as offensive and even harmful to individuals, the community, the state and/or to God. In the Abrahamic religions there are many moral exhortations and legal prohibitions against certain expressions viewed as religiously injurious, in both the foundational scriptures and subsequent jurisprudence. In the Torah, for example, taking the name of the Lord in vain and worshipping false gods or graven images are considered deeply harmful actions, breaking the covenant between God and his people. In Christian Europe, ecclesiastical and temporal authorities took steps to limit religious freedom and harshly punish blasphemy and heresy. In medieval and early modern Christian states, offences against orthodox religious beliefs were often regarded as offences against the temporal state and tantamount to treason, as was the case with Catholics and Protestant Dissenters in England in the 16th and 17th centuries (Nash, 2007: 2–4).

Islamic ideas on freedom of speech

More than any other group, Muslims and Islam are currently often perceived as being 'Other', hostile to freedom of speech and promoting views incompatible with supposed 'Western' values more widely. Thus it is particularly important to pay attention to Islamic thought on freedom of speech.

Millions of Muslims worldwide rely on varying interpretations of Islamic law to guide their conduct. Islamic law consists of a vast corpus of different, often competing, scholarly interpretations of the

Islamic scriptures (the Qu'ran and the Hadith). Through analysing these sources, jurists seek to understand how God wants humans to behave in different situations. There is no single 'law book' for Islamic law, and the interpretations of a particular scholar (issued as *fatwas*, nonbinding legal opinions) are simply that – interpretations, which some Muslims take as authoritative and enforceable, and which others dismiss (Hendrickson, 2013: 173–174). Some Muslim-majority countries today enforce particular understandings of Islamic law through the courts, whereas in Britain, Muslims may follow any interpretation they wish, within the boundaries of the civil law. These points are poorly understood in British media outlets, some of which publish sensationalist stories about Muslim scholars issuing illiberal or restrictive fatwas without making clear that such interpretations have little relevance to most British Muslims (for example Thornhill, 2015).

Two strands of Islamic law are related to freedom of speech: one that restricts certain social-religious expressions (to protect Islam as a faith), and another that protects particular political expressions (to make rulers accountable) (Rabb, 2012: 167). As in other religions, historically Islamic scholars saw freedom of speech as something that is both risky and to be upheld within limits. Jurists condemned blasphemy, and particularly unrepentant apostasy, which was seen as tantamount to threatening the Muslim community. They advised more or less harsh penalties for religiously injurious speech depending on their interpretation of scripture and the context (Rabb, 2012: 158–161). But whilst prohibiting blasphemy, medieval Islamic states offered varying levels of toleration to certain religious minorities – Jews and Christians as 'People of the Book', but also Zoroastrians and, for the Hanafi and Maliki legal schools, other groups like Hindus (Friedmann, 2013: 342–343).

To prevent strife in the political realm, medieval jurists required Muslims to obey their rulers, even tyrannical ones, and discouraged rebellion except in extreme circumstances (Hashmi, 2013: 459). Nonetheless, they provided a certain level of legal protection for political dissent, for example elucidating constraints on rulers' ability to suppress rebels who have a just cause. Rabb sees the defence of the right to rebel as analogous to a modern defence of political speech that criticises governments. She argues, however, that this Islamic right to reasonable dissent is suppressed in authoritarian Muslim-majority states today. She also notes the exaggeration of blasphemy laws for political purposes or to settle scores, as with the high-profile case of Pakistani Christian Asia Bibi (Rabb, 2012: 148–151; 167).

Some Islamic scholars today argue that freedom of speech is rooted deeply within Islamic law. Kamali recommends that a balance needs to be struck between modern commitments to democracy and the classical Islamic legal tradition, which protected political dissent. In his book *Freedom of Expression in Islam*, he argues that Islamic law encourages freedom of speech as long as it is based upon affirmative evidence and is underpinned by freedom of belief for all within Islam. He insists the individual right to formulate and express opinions is guaranteed under Qur'anic principles (Kamali, 1997: 26).

Yet such guarantees may not always be upheld. Khalid Abou El Fadl, a contemporary Islamic legal scholar, offers a consideration of those authoritarian approaches to thinking and speaking that create extremist trends socially and religiously and their implications for modern education. He critiques authoritarian approaches to Islamic law that can be found in some manifestations of Islam today and uses this analysis to explain totalitarian authoritarianism in Saudi Arabia (Abou El Fadl, 2001, 2014). Against the backdrop of extremisms (both secular and religious) that curtail debate and assert the validity of only one interpretation, his work shows better alternatives: the importance and value of choice when interpreting religious texts (although some challenge his lack of engagement with Hadith literature). As Slater shows, Abou El Fadl uses 'strategic hesitancy' to avoid the curtailment of discourse (Slater, 2016).

Spinoza: the liberty to philosophise

In the medieval and early modern periods, speech was often curtailed, but in certain circumstances (as in some aspects of Islamic law) limited freedom of speech and religious freedoms were upheld. It was in this context that new ideas about the importance of freedom of speech and freedom of religion emerged in Europe.

Writing after the violence of the Thirty Years' War, the Jewish Dutch philosopher Baruch Spinoza (1632–1677) was one of the first modern European thinkers to focus upon freedom of speech. In *Tractatus Theologico-Politicus* (1670), which sought to challenge the political power wielded by religious authorities, he provided a liberal justification for the protection of freedom of speech and freedom of religion. This is rooted in his argument that everyone has an inalienable natural right to think what they like and make up their minds about difficult issues, including religion, and that the 'most tyrannical governments are those which make crimes of opinions' (Spinoza, 1670: 241). He argued that people 'cannot, without disastrous results, be compelled to speak only according to the dictates' of the government (Spinoza, 1670: 258). Any government's attempts to constrain freedom of speech would only undermine its own authority, by inspiring people to revolt (Spinoza, 1670: 261–262).

Spinoza acknowledged that speech sometimes leads to harmful social consequences, and that governments might have to restrict certain speech to preserve peace (Spinoza, 1670: 258). But overall, he insisted, any harm caused by freedom of speech is greatly outweighed by the beneficial consequences in terms of human knowledge and progress:

> [Such freedom] is absolutely necessary for progress in science and the liberal arts: for no man follows such pursuits to advantage unless his judgment be entirely free and unhampered.
>
> (Spinoza, 1670: 261)

Spinoza's lasting relevance for these debates is his combination of ideological (natural rights) and pragmatic (consequentialist and utilitarian) arguments for wide-ranging freedom to speak. These types of argument inform some modern liberal approaches to free speech.

Kant: the immorality of lying

Among the various justifications for freedom of speech, two dominant arguments are 'from truth' and 'from autonomy'. We interpret the right to autonomy as meaning we should be free to act independent of constraint – which, for many theorists historically and today, is a supreme value. Since the Enlightenment, different combinations of these arguments from truth and autonomy have been made by thinkers coming from very different starting points. We see this by comparing the arguments of the German philosopher Immanuel Kant (1724–1804) with those of the English utilitarian philosopher John Stuart Mill (1806–1873).

Kant offered both political and moral arguments in support of freedom of speech. 'Freedom of the pen', he argued, 'is the sole shield of popular rights' (Kant, 1974: 72). It is also the basis for the legitimacy of any government, which depends on how far it represents the people's will; if the government curtails freedom of speech it cannot know the people's will, thus undermining its own authority (Varden, 2010: 49–50). Kant's moral theory also makes a case for open, truthful speech. He argued in *Groundwork for the Metaphysics of Morals* (first published in 1785) that lying is wrong, regardless of the consequences.

Lying to someone violates their autonomy because they lose control of their reasoning processes – they are manipulated to pursue the speaker's objectives rather than their own (Kant, 2002: 47–48). Lying also violates Kant's principle for assessing the morality of actions, the 'categorical imperative': 'Act only in accordance with that maxim through which you can at the same time will that it become a universal law' (Kant, 2002: 37). When considering an action, one should imagine that everyone is behaving in the same way; if a contradiction arises from this thought experiment (either in logic or because no rational being would want the outcome), then the action is immoral. Thus lying is deemed immoral because if universalised it would create a logically impossible situation (if everyone lies, we cannot distinguish lies from truth) (Kant, 2002: 39). Kant's position has clear implications for speech: we have a duty to speak to each other truthfully.

In a 20th-century continuation of Kant, David Strauss (1991) promotes a 'persuasion principle'. He argues that apart from exceptional circumstances, a government must not 'suppress speech on the ground that it is too persuasive' and may lead listeners to accept views of which it (the government) disapproves, because this is an attempt to control the listeners' reasoning, violating their autonomy. Strauss leans towards libertarianism. He concedes this principle may protect manipulative private speech (even expressions of racial or religious hatred) from state intervention, but argues that it would not protect clearly false statements because government restriction of lies does more good than harm (Strauss, 1991: 354–362).

Mill: the harm principle

Writing at a time of popular agitation for greater democracy across Europe, John Stuart Mill was concerned with preserving the freedom of the individual and the group from the majority's dominance. In *On Liberty* (first published in 1859), he offered a consequentialist argument 'from truth'. He argued that freedom of speech must be as wide as possible, no matter how marginal, immoral or false someone's view might be, because it is essential for helping people to find the truth and hold government to account. Mill believed that freedom of speech should be understood as a collective, co-operative process – people cannot be sure whether they are correct in their understanding of truth, so they must be free to talk with others to explore as many views as possible to reach truths that will benefit all (Mill, 1869: 31–99).

Mill's maximalist approach to freedom of speech, and individual freedom more widely, includes 'the harm principle': 'the only purpose for which power can be rightfully exercised over any member of a civilized community, against his will, is to prevent harm to others' (Mill, 1869: 22). He argued that an individual's freedom can only legitimately be constrained by government if that person's actions are likely to harm someone else or their rights. By 'harmful' speech, he meant language which is clearly likely to incite *imminent* physical violence against others (Mill, 1869). Since Mill's time, however, there has been considerable debate about what actually constitutes sufficient harm to justify state curtailment of freedom of speech.

Dworkin and Barendt: liberal arguments against suppressing hate speech

Spinoza, Kant and Mill argued in varying degrees that we should each strive to be ethical, control our use of freedom of speech for the sake of the general good, and expect our government to support us in this. But the contexts in which they made their defences of freedom of speech (appealing to autonomy and truth) have now changed dramatically. Ideas about truth have become more relative through the centuries: even a scientific realist has to admit that new discoveries can change the way we understand the material world, let alone our understandings of different moralities and belief systems. Moreover, in recent decades new interpretations of what counts as 'harm' have emerged in debates about restrictions on speech. The term 'hate speech' gained traction in the 1980s and 1990s, with Matsuda (1993) warning about the dangers of racism on American university campuses, which remains highly relevant.

By contrast, some modern liberal political philosophers lean even harder on the right to autonomy as a defence of freedom of speech, by assuming that we have free will, to a greater or lesser degree, and that governments should not inhibit free use of speech, even hate speech. The American scholar Ronald Dworkin (1931–2013) exemplified this. He asserted that our individual right to speak freely trumps other considerations and recommended that, as a rule of thumb, we can use insult and mockery when we see fit.[2] For him, hate speech bans undermine citizens' political agency (and the legitimacy of democracy) by denying them the capacity to contest the laws that govern them (Dworkin, 1994; Gould, 2019: 172–173).

Dworkin's argument aligns broadly with what we call the *liberal approach* to freedom of speech (see Table 1.1), which defends that freedom even for offensive views. Dworkin even tends towards libertarian views. Another theorist who broadly shares this approach, while not advocating insult and mockery, is Eric Barendt. Writing in response to UK plans to criminalise the glorification of terrorism, Barendt takes a consequentialist approach, arguing that it may be of educational value to society to permit people who glorify terrorism to express their views publicly, so that the public can interrogate why they think this way. He also cites the 'danger that if extreme speech is not tolerated, it will be driven underground' (Barendt, 2005: 898).

Liberal approaches often assume (akin to Mill) that a group of citizens can come to shared understanding of truth through free public debate (the justification 'from truth'). An exaggerated form of this is reflected in the phrase enshrined in American law of the 'marketplace of ideas' (Schultz, 2009): the belief that ideas, like money, should be free to circulate, survive or fail, by analogy with the economic free trade model. This analogy assumes that if ideas are given free rein, the best argument will win; more speech will remedy 'bad' speech. This view is a common feature of libertarianism. Yet it ignores other factors such as power differentials and the harm that speech can cause, and can be used in neoliberal justifications of free speech, which actually serve to cement the position of people who exercise power over more vulnerable ones.

Waldron: guarded liberalism drifting towards no-platforming

Jeremy Waldron takes an opposing view; he attempts to expand Mill's definition of harm beyond immediate, physical danger. In *The Harm in Hate Speech* (2012), Waldron proposes that people who use hate speech cause real harm by compromising the dignity of others; they are saying '[t]he time for your degradation and your exclusion by the society that presently shelters you is fast approaching' (2012: 96). He wants more restrictions on hate speech than are allowed under the First Amendment to the American Constitution and advocates stronger hate speech legislation such as is found in countries like the United Kingdom.

Risk aversion towards offensive speech aligns with what we call the *guarded liberal* approach. By calling for new laws to prohibit hate speech, Waldron drifts beyond guarded liberalism towards *no-platforming* (see Table 1.1). In calling for new legislation in America, Waldron seeks to protect liberal democratic ideas of equality, dignity and personal independence (autonomy) and sees no usefulness in offensive speech. He differs in this from Mill, who advocated speech that could be a challenge to the 'deep slumber of a decided opinion' (Mill, 1869: 78).

Waldron provides a useful corrective to Mill's liberal view that only physical injury, not verbal insult, is the location of harm (McConnell,

2012). Yet his argument can lead to forms of no-platforming, where people whose views are deemed offensive or harmful are denied access to public platforms (such as university events) from which to speak.

Butler: resist no-platforming with guarded liberalism

At this juncture we turn to philosopher Judith Butler, who emphasises the importance of the human voice. She presents a very different guarded liberal position from that of Waldron, seeking to avoid no-platforming if at all possible. Taking a feminist approach that is different from the mostly white male scholars already discussed, Butler analyses the performativity of our speech acts. We *perform* through language that which we believe to be our identity, through habit and cultural norms (Butler, 1993: 13), and so we daily and repeatedly endorse and perpetuate in language the identities that we learn from our cultural surroundings; and this has a gendered dimension (Butler, 1997: 272). Butler argues that the way we perform speech acts means that speech is not merely a vehicle for expressing our identities and ideas, but also a process by which they are actively constructed.

Butler acknowledges the destructive power of hate speech but does not think the state should restrict it to protect vulnerable people or minorities. Instead, she shows the necessity of discussing the painful and difficult accusations that people bring against each other, rather than suppressing or censoring them (Butler, 1997). This should not be seen as support of the so-called lesser harm argument whereby speech deserves special protection because it does less harm than physical blows (Schauer, 1993: 641). Like Sorial, discussed following, Butler accepts that speech can do great harm, both indirectly and directly, and believes it would be naïve to argue that if we permit hate speech, we will always be able to defuse it. Nonetheless, she criticises state prohibition of hate speech, arguing that this can lead inadvertently to hateful expressions being propagated far and wide in media coverage; this makes it more difficult to dismantle their power (Butler, 1997: 38). She argues that if left uncensored, hurtful words can be turned against the aggressor once they are accepted and acknowledged in their truly powerful form:

> The word that wounds becomes an instrument of resistance in the redeployment that destroys the prior territory of its operation.
> (Butler, 1997: 163)

Thus, despite acknowledging that the personal risks to the victim outweigh those to the perpetrator, she counsels against no-platforming.

Ricoeur: who are you actually talking to?

Although he did not understand this feminist approach, Paul Ricoeur (1913–2005) worked a great deal on communicating with others and asked: who are you actually speaking to? Ricoeur insisted that we should try to understand and take ownership of ideas we disagree with, in order to attempt some resolution. This is a form of linguistic hospitality that helps us to be conciliatory while not abandoning our principles.

Ricoeur hoped that a mutual labour of understanding would lead us to use language ethically:

> All speech acts ... commit their speaker through a tacit pledge of sincerity by reason of which I actually mean what I say. Simple assertion involves this commitment: I believe that what I say is true and I offer my belief to others so that they too will share it.
> (Ricoeur, 1991: 217)

This sounds both naïve and libertarian, but it resembles more closely the liberal or guarded liberal approaches. Ricoeur is very different from the thinkers so far discussed, because for him, speaking is a form of moral action that necessitates us taking responsibility for speaking to others and trying to understand their position. He also warns against the author of a speech action presenting themselves as ethically neutral, which he thinks is impossible. We argue in Chapter 7 that these ideas about the obligations that participants in a discussion have to each other are important for building a culture of reciprocity in universities.

In a liberal democracy, liberal thought is expected to be the umpire between two assumptions: one is that we are all rational and similar (universalism), and the other is that we are all different (relativism). While Dworkin leaned towards universalism, Ricoeur believed that upholding both assumptions simultaneously (despite the inevitable complexity) is infinitely preferable to Dworkin's approach, which he understood as one side of a sterile oppositional argument (Ricoeur, 1992: 57; 287).

Fish and Sorial: freedom of speech is not a core academic value

In order to try to resolve the existential contradiction at the heart of liberal thought between universalism and relativism, some, like Dworkin, have turned to rights-based arguments. But the public intellectual Stanley Fish counsels against this. In contrast to rights-based approaches, Fish sees it as unrealistic to treat freedom of speech as a right or a principle, because such absolutism cannot be enforced. He understands freedom of speech to be a value (which may be relative, context-dependent and open to contestation) rather than a right (which makes the concept seem immutable and raises unrealistic hopes that it can be fully enforceable by law) (Fish, 2019).

Writing about the American context, Fish challenges the First Amendment, which protects freedom of speech much more than UK law. In *There's No Such Thing as Free Speech, and It's a Good Thing, Too* (1994), he argues that all speech is constrained in some way because it is only within the constraining contexts of communities that speech becomes intelligible 'assertion rather than noise' (Fish, 1994: 115). Talk about 'freedom of speech' is misplaced because such a thing is impossible – there is no neutral space without constraints on speech. As such, he argues against making appeals to freedom of speech to protect particular speech acts; instead, whether particular expressions should be permitted or prohibited should be decided on a case-by-case basis.

In the university context, Fish argues that academia does not, in fact, give everyone the right to speak freely; routinely, it encourages expert voices over the unqualified. He rejects the automatic assumption that 'education is enhanced when there is more speech' and believes universities should not be obliged to host every speaker requested by students and staff. He also thinks that because universities' prime mission is education, they should avoid taking 'political' stances and stick to campus matters in their public pronouncements (Fish, 2019: 63–87).

Fish appears to embrace two extremes; both libertarian and no-platforming. In a libertarian manner, he asserts, for example, that the American academic Amy Wax, who holds controversial views about immigrants, should not have been taken off her first-year undergraduate teaching duties (Fish, 2019: 87–94). Wax adopts a form of 'cultural distance nationalism', recommending that immigrants who share 'American values' should be preferred to those who do not (*The Federalist*, 2019). Fish defends her right to express this position, although it can be argued that she is voicing an opinion that is, by his own definition, *political*. Wax has strong views on off-campus issues, that can be understood as offensive and raising issues of racism. It is also significant that Fish makes no suggestion that students should be encouraged to challenge Wax about her views, which we see as vital to rectify the democratic deficit we identify in later chapters. As a libertarian pragmatist, Fish defends Wax's right to express her controversial position on migrants and yet, as a no-platformer, he advocates that universities should avoid certain kinds of speech in order to avoid political engagement.

Fish's view has some synergy with that of Sarah Sorial, who also rejects the idea that freedom of speech is 'valued above all else' in academia (Sorial, 2012: 176). She too is sceptical of liberal defences of extreme speech (Sorial, 2010: 287). She shares Butler's criticism of hate speech bans, but not her disagreement with no-platforming. Instead, Sorial advocates that institutions should take responsibility for tackling hate speech because it is often by speaking at places like universities that extremists secure legitimacy. She places negative duties upon universities, which include delegitimising extreme views by, for example, refusing to host them. Yet Sorial also identifies positive duties for institutions like universities, including the need to contest extreme views (such as by calling out hate speech expressed in the classroom) and to support oppressed groups (Sorial, 2012: 165; 178).

Hankinson Nelson, Habermas and Peirce: community approaches

Finally, we turn to three theorists who are not so much concerned with freedom of speech, as with the process of learning with others.

Lynn Hankinson Nelson argues that it is not individuals who generate new knowledge, but groups: 'evidence is communal' (Hankinson Nelson, 1993: 137). She uses the term 'epistemological communities' to convey this belief. This resonates with Mill's invitation to individuals to group together and hammer out new ways forward. It also gives us a different way of thinking about rules on handling freedom of speech. Instead of the state-given rules for which Kant argued, a community-centred approach encourages us to decide for ourselves what the limits or liberties of freedom of speech should be, within our own institutions.

Meanwhile, Jürgen Habermas, the German philosopher and public intellectual, reflects on the limits that liberal democracies require for particular kinds of speech – religious reasoning – in public debate in a multifaith, postsecular society. He argues that the secular state may propose that it is liberal and neutral but that these are elusive and possibly impossible qualities: secularism is a necessary yet insufficient condition for guaranteeing religious freedom for everyone (Habermas, 2006: 4). He considers whether religious citizens are forced to shoulder an excessive, asymmetric burden because they have to translate their political arguments into secular language that is (assumed to be) neutral and accessible to all. Whilst arguing that untranslated religious reasoning *should* be permitted in public debate (though not within formal political institutions like Parliaments), he concludes that there is an equally onerous (but necessary) cognitive burden upon secular citizens. In a postsecular society where religion persists, liberal citizenship demands both that people recognise 'the limits of secular reason', *and* that they reject the outright 'exclusion of religious doctrines from the genealogy of reason' (Habermas, 2006: 15–16). This reciprocity of obligations on religious and secular citizens requires what he calls 'complementary learning processes' (Habermas, 2006: 16). However, Habermas accepts the impossibility of success for such processes. He decides that a precondition of success for a liberal secular state involves the acceptance that these complementary learning processes are both vitally important and impossible to achieve: we will never fully understand and accept each other. We view universities as the place for such learning struggles, and this is what tames political power and makes peaceful coexistence possible. We propose that modern multifaith universities cannot expect their students to make arguments only through (translated) secular language; to avoid an excessive burden on religious students, there must be some accommodation in the classroom for religious-based reasoning.

Recognising the reciprocal obligations on participants in a debate is an essential part of the 'Community of Inquiry' (CofI). This pedagogy is a form of community-centred learning developed by the pragmatist philosopher C.S. Peirce (1839–1914), who sought to create a learning environment where divisive issues can be discussed carefully and frankly (Peirce, 1958; Shields, 1999). In this form of managed discussion, participants are encouraged to reflect on their fundamental beliefs and to ask themselves whether they really have a clear understanding of an issue, or simply opinions they wish to protect unchallenged (Pardales and Girod, 2006; Scott-Baumann, 2010). Establishing the CofI requires participants to agree explicitly to the procedures and parameters within which a discussion will be held, giving them ownership of the learning environment. In Chapter 7 we show how this can be applied in the university context to help resolve the free speech wars.

A fourfold model for handling freedom of speech practically

We have seen that a range of philosophical arguments can be made in defence of freedom of speech, even for offensive or hateful speech. Aside from the rights-based argument from autonomy, and the consequentialist argument from truth, other consequentialist justifications include arguments from democracy (that the freedom to convey ideas is necessary so citizens can decide how to govern themselves) (Meiklejohn, 1948), and arguments from suspicion of government (that government suppression of hate speech is a slippery slope and likely to be worse for society than hate speech's expression) (Strauss, 1991: 350). There is also a range of objections to these arguments, and strong claims that hate speech should not be protected (such as from Waldron).

But theoretical considerations only take us so far. How can we summarise different approaches to freedom of speech in a more practical way, to aid universities (and other institutions) in their decision making? We outline four main approaches to freedom of speech, which provide a new paradigm for handling the issue practically. Each approach can be understood both as an *attitude* (a belief about how certain speech acts should be handled), and as a practical *strategy* for handling speech, which can be chosen consciously by organisers of discussions or events (see Table 1.1).

The *liberal approach* prioritises the value of freedom of speech, asserting the right of speakers to speak freely as far as possible within the law, and the right of others to question them to evaluate the probity of their arguments, as Spinoza, Kant and Mill demanded. However, when exaggerated, *liberal* can become *libertarian*. The libertarian approach can sometimes lead to the problematic position of seeing one's right to speak as paramount, to be exercised without real regard for the rights of others. But libertarianism can also be understood as a practical strategy for handling debate in a particular context; it can sometimes be useful for enabling issues to be explored to their fullest extent without any constraint. As strategies, we distinguish between the liberal and the libertarian by focusing not on what people say (both permit the expression of any lawful views), but *how* they say it: libertarianism permits language that may be grossly offensive, but the liberal approach does not. For the purpose of our model, which is to help universities handle speech practically, we restrict both the liberal and libertarian approaches to speech within the law. More widely, of course, some libertarians contest any legal prohibitions on speech.

The *guarded liberal approach* prioritises the protection of others from significant offence. Both as an attitude and a strategy, it is risk-averse. It supports the exercise of freedom of speech but tends to see it primarily through the lens of risk management, as something to be cautious of, rather than as something to be exercised confidently. As a strategy for handling speech events, guarded liberalism means agreeing to certain restrictions designed to reduce the risk of causing offence.

If stretched to its fullest extent, *guarded liberalism* can become *no-platforming*. We use this term more broadly than is commonly used in Higher Education (to describe a decision to turn down a previously invited speaker),[3] to refer to both an attitude to freedom of speech, and a strategy for handling it, where particularly offensive voices or divisive topics are to be barred from the debate.

Within guarded liberalism there are different degrees of willingness to tolerate illiberal views that undermine other people's rights. For example, Waldron's position is guarded liberalism, which can tip over into no-platforming; and Sorial encourages universities to refuse a platform to extreme speakers as a standard practice. Yet Butler's version of guarded liberalism steps back from no-platforming, which she sees as counterproductive.

The fourfold model can used by students, lecturers and students' union officers seeking to establish a CofI, which is necessary to resist risk aversion and build a culture of reciprocity in dialogue (see Chapter 7 and the Appendix).

Conclusion

We have seen how speech debates have shifted over time from being dominated by small numbers of individuals with power, usually white and male, to more egalitarian and often feminist attempts to 'speak truth to power' and challenge racism. For Socrates, Kant and Mill, the speakers and listeners were usually privileged, so there was little need to consider power imbalances between them. For Butler, Matsuda and Sorial, however, the different contexts of speakers and listeners are crucial when considering how best to manage dialogue; sometimes restricting the speech of someone with more power can enhance the freedom of someone with less opportunity to speak. For Habermas, meanwhile, common assumptions of the primacy of secular reasoning need to be displaced to accommodate religious arguments in public debate. He predicts that this will not always lead to improved understanding but it can and must increase the likelihood of complementary learning processes and spread the cognitive burden more evenly, so that all parties make the effort to see the validity of both religious and secular approaches to reasoning.

Different contexts may require different approaches to handling freedom of speech. By using our fourfold model flexibly and (crucially) explicitly and transparently, in dialogue with students, university staff can better navigate the tension between freedom of speech and freedom from harm. We explain this in Chapter 7.

Universities will, however, tend to gravitate towards one position or another as a standard. We recommend pursuing the liberal approach as a default position, only sometimes deviating from this when particular contexts demand it. This would mean confidently upholding

Table 1.1 A fourfold model for handling freedom of speech

Approach	Characteristics	Example in University Context
Liberal ↕	Supports the exercise of freedom of speech as far as possible, and the expression of any views, provided they are within the law. Causing offence not seen as a valid reason to avoid exercise of freedom of speech. But speakers should moderate their language, expressing their view without using expressions that many others will find grossly offensive or hateful.	University/students' union upholds students' request for an external speaker well known for expressing hostile views towards immigrants. Speaker is able to express views on this topic freely. University may ask the speaker in advance to adhere to a code of conduct wherein speakers should avoid expressions that are commonly considered grossly offensive or hateful.
Libertarian	Supports the exercise of freedom of speech as far as possible, and the expression of any views, provided they are within the law. Speakers should be free to use any lawful language they wish, including expressions that others find grossly offensive or hateful.	University/students' union upholds students' request for this speaker. Speaker is able to express views on this topic freely. University does not require the speaker to moderate language or put in place any other restrictions on the speech.
Guarded liberal ↕	Supports exercise of freedom of speech, but not to the point of causing significant offence to others. Risk-averse. Speech may be facilitated but under restrictions designed to reduce risk of offence.	University/students' union may or may not choose to uphold students' request for this speaker. If it does, university imposes mitigating conditions, e.g., requiring an opposing voice on panel, or requiring speaker to submit the speech in advance.
No-platforming	Prioritises protecting people from offence over upholding freedom of speech. Willing to prevent speech events from happening in order to reduce risk of offence. Can include preventing particular people from speaking, or disallowing discussion of particular topics.	University/students' union does not uphold students' request for this speaker.

freedom of speech, including for external speakers with controversial or offensive views. We disagree with those who believe that universities should refuse to host such people in order to delegitimise them. We remain convinced by the various arguments from consequences and autonomy that, on balance, it is better for society that such views are heard, especially in places like universities, which should be encouraging listeners to subject speakers to critical examination. The 'marketplace of ideas' is a flawed concept, and the damage done by offensive speech cannot necessarily be repaired or counterbalanced by opposing speech – but this is not a sufficient reason for justifying the exclusion *by default* of such voices from campus.

Moreover, we believe that a default liberal approach, including for controversial speakers, is necessary to push back against risk aversion among students more widely. It is essential for an effective learning environment that students feel free to express their views as they wish to in class, and do not feel they need overly to self-censor.

Notes

1 See, for example, the Preamble of the Universal Declaration of Human Rights, which draws on the language of 'personalism', a concept promoted heavily in Catholic Social Teaching in the early 20th century (Spencer, 2016: 135–136).
2 Dworkin (2006) seemed to contradict that when he argued that newspapers were correct in refusing to reprint the Danish cartoons of the Prophet Muhammad, but not because he wished to avoid insulting Muslims. His reason was that he believed the incident was orchestrated to increase tensions between the Muslim and the non-Muslim world.
3 The term is used in a more specific way by the National Union of Students (NUS) (2017), to describe its prohibition on its officers from sharing a platform with individuals or organisations with 'racist or fascist views'.

References

Abou El Fadl, K. (2001) *And God Knows the Soldiers: The Authoritative and Authoritarian in Islamic Discourses.* Lanham MD: University Press of America.

Abou El Fadl, K. (2014) *Reasoning with God: Reclaiming Shari'ah in the Modern Age.* Lanham MD: Rowman and Littlefield.

Barendt, E. (2005) 'Threats to Freedom of Speech in the United Kingdom?' *University of New South Wales Law Journal*, 28, 3: 895–899. http://www.austlii.edu.au/au/journals/UNSWLJ/2005/55.html.

Beard, M. (2017) *Women & Power: A Manifesto.* London: Profile Books Ltd.

Butler, J. (1993) *Bodies That Matter: On the Discursive Limits of Sex.* New York: Routledge.

Butler, J. (1997) *Excitable Speech: A Politics of the Performative*. New York: Routledge.
Dworkin, R. (1994) 'A New Map of Censorship', *Index on Censorship*, 1–2: 9–15. https://journals.sagepub.com/doi/10.1080/03064229408535633.
Dworkin, R. (2006) 'The Right to Ridicule', *The New York Review of Books*, 23 March. https://www.nybooks.com/articles/2006/03/23/the-right-to-ridicule/.
Fish, S. (1994) *There's No Such Thing as Free Speech and It's a Good Thing Too*. Oxford: Oxford University Press.
Fish, S. (2019) *The First: How to Think About Hate Speech, Campus Speech, Religious Speech, Fake News, Post-Truth, and Donald Trump*. New York: Atria/One Signal.
Friedmann, Y. (2013) 'Minorities'. In Bowering, G. (ed.) *The Princeton Encyclopedia of Islamic Political Thought*. Princeton, NJ: Princeton University Press: 340–346.
Gould, R.R. (2019) 'Is the "Hate" in Hate Speech the "Hate" in Hate Crime? Waldron and Dworkin on Political Legitimacy', *Jurisprudence*, 10, 2: 171–187.
Habermas, J. (2006) 'Religion in the Public Sphere', *European Journal of Philosophy*, 14, 1: 1–25.
Hankinson Nelson, L. (1993) 'Epistemological Communities'. In Alcoff, L., and Potter, E. (eds.) *Feminist Epistemologies*. New York: Routledge: 121–159.
Hashmi, S.H. (2013) 'Rebellion'. In Bowering, G. (ed.) *The Princeton Encyclopedia of Islamic Political Thought*. Princeton, NJ: Princeton University Press: 459–460.
Hendrickson, J. (2013) 'Fatwa'. In Bowering, G. (ed.) *The Princeton Encyclopedia of Islamic Political Thought*. Princeton, NJ: Princeton University Press: 173–174.
Kamali, M.H. (1997) *Freedom of Expression in Islam*. Cambridge: Islamic Texts Society.
Kant, I. (1974) *On the Old Saw: That May be Right in Theory but It Won't Work in Practice*. Edited by G. Miller and translated by E.B. Ashton. Philadelphia: University of Pennsylvania Press. First published in 1793.
Kant, I. (2002) *Groundwork for the Metaphysics of Morals*. Edited and translated by A.W. Wood. Binghamton, NY: Vail-Ballou Press. First published in 1785.
Matsuda, M.J. (1993) *Words That Wound: Critical Race Theory, Assaultive Speech, and the First Amendment*. Boulder, CO: Westview Press.
McConnell, M.W. (2012) 'You Can't Say That', *New York Times*, 22 January. https://www.nytimes.com/2012/06/24/books/review/the-harm-in-hate-speech-by-jeremy-waldron.html.
Meiklejohn, A. (1948) *Free Speech and Its Relation to Self-Government*. New York: Harper.
Mill, J.S. (1869) *On Liberty*. 4th ed. London: Longmans, Green, Reader and Dyer.
Nash, D. (2007) *Blasphemy in the Christian World: A History*. Oxford: Oxford University Press.

National Union of Students (2017) *NUS' No Platform Policies*. https://www.nusconnect.org.uk/resources/nus-no-platform-policy-f22f.

Pardales, M.J. and Girod, M. (2006) 'Community of Inquiry: Its Past and Present Future', *Educational Philosophy and Theory*, 38, 3: 299–309.

Peirce, C.S. (1958) 'The Fixation of Belief'. In Wiener, P. (ed.) *Charles Sanders Peirce: Selected Writings*. New York: Dover Publications: 91–112.

Rabb, I. (2012) 'Negotiating Speech in Islamic Law and Politics: Flipped Traditions of Expression'. In Emon, A., Ellis, M. and Glahn, B. (eds.) *Islamic Law and International Human Rights Law*. Oxford: Oxford University Press: 144–167.

Ricoeur, P. (1991) *Lectures I: Autour du politique*. Paris: Seuil.

Ricoeur, P. (1992) *Lectures II: La Contrée des philosophes*. Paris: Seuil.

Schauer, F. (1993) 'The Phenomenology of Speech and Harm', *Ethics*, 103, 4: 635–654. https://www.journals.uchicago.edu/doi/pdfplus/10.1086/293546.

Schultz, D. (2009) 'The Marketplace of Ideas', *The First Amendment Encyclopedia*. https://mtsu.edu/first-amendment/article/999/marketplace-of-ideas#:~:text=%20Marketplace%20of%20Ideas%20%201%20Concept%20is,first%20reference%20to%20the%20marketplace%20of...%20More%20.

Scott-Baumann, A. (2010) 'A Community of Inquiry: Talking to Muslims'. In Farrar, M. (ed.) *The Study of Islam within Social Science Curricula in UK Universities: Case Studies 1*. Centre for Sociology, Anthropology and Politics, Higher Education Academy: 81–84. https://www.heacademy.ac.uk/system/files/max_farrar_case_studies.pdf.

Shields, P. (1999) '*The Community of Inquiry: Insights for Public Administration from Jane Addams, John Dewey and Charles S. Peirce*'. Presentation to the *Public Administration Theory Network*, Portland, Oregon, 23–25 March. https://pdfs.semanticscholar.org/bb79/047730c927732945b2dbe21bba13813bbd7a.pdf.

Slater, A. (2016) 'Strategic Hesitancy in the discourse of Khalid Abou El Fadl: Sources and Implementation', *ReOrient: The Journal of Critical Muslim Studies*, 1, 3: 293–321.

Sorial, S. (2010) 'Can Saying Something Make It So? The Nature of Seditious Harm', *Law and Philosophy*, 29, 3: 273–305. https://link.springer.com/article/10.1007/s10982-009-9063-0.

Sorial, S. (2012) *Sedition and the Advocacy of Violence: Free Speech and Counter-Terrorism*. London: Routledge.

Spencer, N. (2016) *The Evolution of the West*. London: Society for Promoting Christian Knowledge.

Spinoza, B. (1670) *Tractatus Theologico-Politicus*. Amsterdam: Jan Rieuwertsz.

Strauss, D.A. (1991) 'Persuasion, Autonomy, and Freedom of Expression', *Columbia Law Review*, 91: 334–371. https://core.ac.uk/download/pdf/207571931.pdf.

The Federalist (2019) 'Here's What Amy Wax Really Said about Immigration', *The Federalist*, 26 July. https://thefederalist.com/2019/07/26/heres-amy-wax-really-said-immigration/.

Thornhill, T. (2015) 'They've Really Got the Hump! Fatwa Declared against Snowmen Made to Look Like Camels and Arabs in Saudi as They "Represent Western Values"', *MailOnline*, 12 January. https://www.dailymail.co.uk/news/article-2906866/They-ve-really-got-hump-Fatwa-declared-against-snowmen-look-like-camels-Arabs-Saudi-represent-Western-values.html.

Varden, H. (2010) 'A Kantian Conception of Free Speech'. In Golash, D. (ed.) *Free Speech in a Diverse World*. New York: Springer: 39–55.

Waldron, J. (2012) *The Harm in Hate Speech*. Cambridge, MA: Harvard University Press.

2 Populism, freedom of speech and human rights

Freedom of speech wars on campus do not occur in a vacuum but are shaped by wider political upheavals, of which two have great impact on these debates. First, there is a rise in mass movements (often called 'populist') in the United Kingdom, the United States and Europe. Second, there is a rise in feelings of entitlement to personal rights: online and offline people often appeal to their personal right to speak freely in ways that disregard and challenge the rights of others (such as the right to live free from fear of hatred and harm).

In this chapter we examine the connections between populism, freedom of speech and human rights. The United Kingdom uses an uneasy combination of liberal democracy and rights-based liberalism to decide what it thinks about freedom of speech. On the one hand, liberal democracy presumes that we are each autonomous as long as what we do is protected by laws. On the other hand, rights-based liberalism appeals to a higher belief that we all have universal human rights. The difficulty here is how to balance competing needs and rights: at any one time, the law must decide in favour of one person's rights over those of another, and so not all rights can be exercised equally, simultaneously or to their full extent. In addition, the capitalism at the core of liberal democracy entails inequality that extreme groups can exploit. Right-wing populism sneaks into the gap between liberal democracy and rights-based liberalism and plays libertarian and no-platforming demands off against each other, inhibiting free speech by creating adversarial, antagonistic positions.

To explore these issues, we begin by examining the concept of populism and its key features. Then we explore how right-wing populist leaders gain power by making cynical appeals to free speech rights, sometimes to justify their Islamophobia. Claims about universities and students form an important part of their rhetorical arsenal. Finally, we consider populist hate speech and student attempts to resist it by no-platforming speakers who, for example, they consider racist. We show how right-wing populism distorts human rights principles of freedom of expression *and* liberal democratic aspirations to freedom of speech, and we suggest deliberative democracy, the development of group work to share and solve problems, as a powerful response.

What is populism?

One problem when trying to understand populism is the diverse range of people and movements to whom the label 'populist' is applied. They include those on the political right, such as Donald Trump, anti-European Union political parties and grassroots far-right movements such as that led by Tommy Robinson; those on the political left, such as Momentum (part of the UK Labour Party) and grassroots movements like Occupy Wall Street; and movements that seem to break out of the traditional right/left binary like Leave.EU. Some theorists look for similarities among phenomena identified as populist. We analyse three approaches to focus upon two major characteristics: populism as a movement that polarises people's understanding of politics into binaries such as 'us v them', and populism as a movement that relies more upon powerful emotive language than upon ideology or planning. We understand 'ideology' as a systematic ordering of ideas to justify actions, inevitably creating exaggeration in order to make the ideas seem real (Ricoeur, 1976; Scott-Baumann, 2017).

The first, explanatory, approach to populism, often known as the ideational approach, focuses on analysing the ideas shared by populism's different forms. This provides an understanding of populism as commonly sharing three simple claims:

1. Society is divided into binaries, such as 'us v them' and 'the people v the elite'
2. The 'people' are pure with a shared, identifiable 'general will', whose needs are not being met
3. The ruling political 'elites' are corrupt and must be ousted (Mudde and Rovira Kaltwasser, 2017; Hawkins et al., 2019: 3)

Understood in this way, populism is a 'thin-centred' ideology that is parasitic upon other, more easily recognisable political movements like socialism and fascism and, most commonly at present, upon liberal democracy. Populist movements promise, falsely, to champion the will of the people and overturn the self-interested governing elite (Baker, 2019).

The second, activist, approach to populism is very different, seeing populism as politics itself, rather than something separate from the usual way of doing politics in a democracy (Laclau, 2005; Mouffe, 2013). In this view, the popular impulse must be respected because conflict is inherent in politics, and there is always an 'us' made up of people without power agitating against 'them', those who have power (Baker, 2019). Laclau and Mouffe, who adopt this approach, propose a new form of populism that the people will construct and that will be emancipatory: populism for them means that the people will take control of their destiny and construct fair political structures. They argue that negative depictions of right-wing populism ignore the fact that populist tendencies underpin all large-group movements, across the political spectrum and not only on the right (Laclau, 2005: 19). Laclau's and Mouffe's work is often called constructivism because they believe any social group can construct a new and better society.

The third, predictively pessimistic, approach to populism is exemplified by Müller (2016), who alerts us to the dangers that he sees ahead. Deeply suspicious of all populist movements, Müller warns that the terms right and left do not help us to understand populism. For example, he shows that Podemos, the Spanish left-wing movement, is inspired by the right-wing political theorist and Nazi sympathiser Carl Schmitt (1988). Schmitt is known for theorising 'decisionism' – the idea that we should support laws made by a government because they are made by the government, not because they are good or appropriate. Agamben (2005) showed how this can lead to the 'state of exception', whereby laws are passed that justify exceptional state control in difficult circumstances and can then be retained after the state of exception is over. Müller (2016) sees this as characteristic of populist parties like Podemos, considering it anti-pluralist, against citizen participation and internally authoritarian. Schmitt would approve of this approach to politics. Indeed, the Podemos leaders, Íñigo Errejón and Pablo Iglesias, have been profoundly influenced by Schmitt, and the risks of Schmitt's legacy that Müller sees in Podemos are plausible. Yet it is possible to interpret Schmitt's legacy more positively; both Podemos leaders have been influenced by Laclau and Mouffe, and Schmitt's ideas about the need for strong leadership and clear decision making could even help to reinvigorate democracy in Spain, if conjoined with good political planning (Booth and Baert, 2018).

All three analyses agree that populist movements often revolve around a charismatic leader. Indeed, in the last decade leaders who bear some of the identikit features of populist leaders have come to power. For example, Donald Trump in the United States, Jair Bolsonaro in Brazil, Viktor Orbán in Hungary and (to some extent) Boris Johnson in the United Kingdom all make strong use of populist rhetoric and display decisionism – making decisions because that shows leadership, regardless of the quality of the decision or its feasibility. In fact, the decisions they make are often based on whipping up emotions and dividing the people rather than offering realistic solutions. Populist leaders have also mismanaged the COVID-19 pandemic, with unclear strategies for protecting citizens from the virus. According to systematic analysis by Garikipati and Kambhampati (2020), female (nonpopulist) leaders, such as Jacinda Ardern and Angela Merkel, have managed COVID-19 better through their proactive policies, effective use of communication and clear appreciation of the risk posed by the virus.

Populist language

Laclau (2005: 10–12) suggests that populist movements are, first and foremost, expressions of the people's will and therefore a clear and powerful expression of political fact. He considers emotive, powerful language that can bind people together to be vital for politics in general and rejects the argument of Minogue (1969) that populist movements rely on distorted rhetoric. Laclau argues that Minogue's position represents the common tendency for 'ethical denigration' of populism. He critiques this idea, also seen in mass psychology analyses, of viewing the individual as potentially reasonable and the crowd as irrational. He argues that features ascribed to populism are inherent in human actions and that analysis of populism therefore provides a way to understand human actions and thoughts (Laclau, 2005: 30; 67). Mouffe (2013, 2014) also proposes that all political discourse relies upon antagonisms that are impossible to resolve and must therefore be replaced with agonism – positive attempts to resolve conflict. Deliberative democracy resembles Mouffe's agonistic approach, and in 2019 Chwalisz (2019) celebrated 'a new wave of contemporary deliberative democracy, based on the premise that political decisions should be the result of reasonable discussion among citizens'.

Laclau and Mouffe's analysis of the power of language (discourse) in popular movements is helpful. They see all discourse as a structured totality that always includes social, political, cultural (and we add gendered) components. Meanwhile, in Europe, we currently see little left-wing populist discourse of the sort that Laclau hoped for. Instead we find populist use of rhetoric that is anti-immigrant and anti-Muslim.

Such hate speech has found a natural home on the internet (KhosraviNik and Unger, 2016; Pohjonen, 2018). Social media platforms are 'distributed, non-hierarchical and democratic', with content generated by people who are suspicious of mainstream media outlets (Bartlett, 2014: 106). It is well evidenced that social media algorithms will multiply postings that evoke strong emotion, and hate speech is effective at that (Pajnik and Sauer, 2019). As Ebner (2020) points out, online extremists have huge influence, and technology firms exploit their power to attract attention. Humans are addicted to the internet: Myerson (2001) noted the inevitable loss in communication of face-to-face, co-present bodies. This online loss of human texture, as Habermas explained it, means that less and less of life is explored through the dialogue in which one seeks to be understood by others. Social media invites us to 'register our desires' through one-sided statements and posts, more than to communicate in a dialogical, balanced way (Myerson, 2001: 32–34).

Mainstream newspapers also repeat populists' language, which is antagonistic and encourages conflicts 'for which no rational solution could ever exist' (Mouffe, 2013: 3). For example, in 2015 the *Daily Express*, a mainstream tabloid that opposes UK membership of the European Union (EU), quoted in detail a speech given by British politician and Brexiteer Nigel Farage in the European Parliament. Farage warned that Turkey would soon become a member of the EU and that millions of Turks would therefore flood into Britain (Burman, 2015). Such emotive assertions were crucial to Farage's target to get the United Kingdom out of the EU. After years of austerity in Britain that made millions desperate for a change of politics, by deploying such rhetoric Farage was able to turn people's desire for domestic change into a debate about the EU.

Green's (2019) analysis of 'bullshit' explains this process. Bullshit is an extreme statement that is so difficult to refute that it becomes unfalsifiable, even if it is untrue, and we are put into the weak position of negating it ('Turkey will not enter the EU, millions of Turks will not come to UK'), which simply repeats the original claim and thereby strengthens it. Green uses Frankfurt's definition of bullshit as being worse than lies (which deny truth) because bullshit denies the very importance of truth (Frankfurt, 1986: 15). Green analyses various forms of bullshit that are very powerful (bullshit as sincerity, as symbolism, and as unfalsifiability). He shows how sincerity trumps accuracy (in our example, Farage may seem sincere when being righteously indignant); symbolism trumps meaning (the Union Jack flag, the plucky little Brits against fat, corrupt Brussels); and unfalsifiability trumps facts (Turkey will not soon enter the EU but most people will not bother to check this). We can also see in Farage's speech the powerful rhetorical techniques proposed by Aristotle: ethos ('trust me'), logos ('believe me') and pathos ('follow me').

Monologic, emotive, exclusionary and loud use of language is a recurring and important feature of (right-wing) populism, which Le Bon describes as 'affirmation without proof as a way of lying' (Laclau, 2005: 27). In extreme cases, populist rhetoric can inspire fear and hate, unilaterally authorising itself to offend on the assumption that the majority of citizens are being deprived of their rights by a dangerous minority. Ricoeur understood how effective this negativity can be, tapping into a human tendency to describe one's personal situation by loss, lack and longing rather than by what we *have* (Scott-Baumann, 2013). This negative approach also relies upon creating binaries that are irreconcilable, as we see in United Kingdom with the Brexit debate between 'Remainers' and 'Leavers'.

The 'people', the 'elite' and empty signifiers

The term 'the people' is much discussed in populist discourse. Butler (2015: 155–156) notes that when a group self-identifies as 'we, the people', they are not doing what they assert, i.e., bonding themselves to the mass of a population. Rather, they are achieving the opposite, by tacitly identifying themselves as special and exclusive, and contrasting themselves with another group that disagrees with them. Green shows how the term 'the people' is used by populists to sharpen differences ('us v them'), isolate their opponents, mobilise diffuse interests and persuade listeners to view themselves as 'the people', as opposed to 'the elites' (Müller, 2016: 261; Green, 2019: 10).

Indeed 'the people' and 'the elite' may not mean much, and yet it is precisely this poverty of meaning that makes them so powerful. Laclau calls these terms 'empty signifiers'. Commentators can use them to appeal to audiences without clarifying their meaning because they are freighted with heavy emotional baggage that renders them hard to refute (Laclau, 2005). The term 'freedom of speech' in populist rhetoric and even in everyday discussion is often an empty signifier, thereby inhibiting constructive proposals for how to handle speech practically. 'Populism', too, can be an empty signifier. As Baker (2019) points out, some politicians and commentators accuse their opponents of being 'populists', in order to delegitimise their arguments and position them as being outside normal politics, and as potential threats to democracy.

Of course, all political figures use rhetorical approaches to appeal to their followers, as Leone (2013) and Leone et al. (2015) show with their close analysis of Barack Obama's style of speech. Obama is not a right-wing populist, yet he uses rhetorical techniques and autobiographical narratives to secure support by appealing to inclusive and empowering emotions of solidarity across class and colour. Here also are empty signifiers, such as 'hope' and 'change we can believe in' (Kumar, 2014). By contrast, right-wing populism's most powerful feature is language that is exclusionary, discriminatory and often racist. Laclau challenges us to use language powerfully, while avoiding bullshit. As we show in Chapter 7, the Community of Inquiry (CofI) approach can be used to challenge the simplistic binaries of populist rhetoric.

Populist leaders, appeals to 'freedom of speech' and Islamophobia

Populism today, particularly on the right, is intricately linked to rhetoric about rights and freedom of speech. Indeed, the phrase 'freedom of speech' has become a rhetorical touchstone for political leaders seeking to present themselves on the side of 'the people'. Boris Johnson demonstrated this in his first speech as prime minister, when he invoked the Union Jack flag: 'It stands for freedom and free speech and habeas corpus and the rule of law'. Johnson promised he would be 'answering at last the plea of the forgotten people and left behind towns' (PoliticsHome, 2019). This approach played into the populist story because, as explained by Philip Alston, United Nations Special Rapporteur on extreme poverty and human rights, this 'left behind' label ensures that 'the majority in society suspect that they have no stake in the human rights enterprise, and that the human rights groups really are just working for "asylum seekers", "felons", "terrorists" and the like' (Alston, 2017: 6).

A common move of populist leaders is to claim that free speech is under attack by 'the elite', or by Muslims, and that they are its defenders. Sometimes they present themselves cynically as victims of censorship – a move that inevitably secures them widespread media coverage. Deploying the rhetoric of freedom of speech under threat has become a way for populist politicians to mask their own power, whilst simultaneously cementing it. Furthermore, for right-wing populists in particular, rhetorical appeals to freedom of speech go hand in hand with attacks on minority groups, particularly immigrants and Muslims. Schmitt (1988) argued that in order to be strong, a nation must be homogenous, which in his view necessitated creation of a friend/enemy dichotomy to unify the state. This involves making difference seem like risk so that minority groups in a majority population can be made to seem dangerous. Religion, culture or skin colour provide easy, visible markers for such othering. When accusing Muslims of being dangerous and a threat to the West, populist leaders are tactically encouraging this friend/enemy dichotomy. This is a version of the inductive fallacy: some terrorists have been Muslim so all Muslims are potential terrorists. Islamophobic speech is another tool by which populists can signal their membership of 'the people'.

Appeals to freedom of speech and Islamophobia merge when populists repeat the long-standing Orientalist claim that Islam censors freedom of speech and thus goes against the rights of liberal, secular society. Commentators who adopt a secular position often cite the Rushdie Affair (1988–9) and the Charlie Hebdo terrorist attack (2015) as proof of the claim that Islam denies freedom of speech in contrast to Western liberal values (Myre, 2019). As Western secularisation continues and affiliation to traditional religious identities declines, values like freedom of speech become sacred principles seen by many as something that cannot be compromised. Muslims can therefore be portrayed by others as censorious and anti-freedom of speech, and if they express concern about speech acts they find offensive, their concerns are dismissed as anti-Western. In the *Re/presenting Islam on Campus* research (see Chapter 4), a senior white female academic showed her class one of the cartoons of the Prophet Muhammad originally published by Danish newspaper Jyllands-Posten in 2005, in order to explain how they had led to feelings of offence and rioting among Muslims globally. A Muslim student made a formal complaint. According to the academic:

> His argument was that I had sort of forced him to break his faith by putting the images up in his presence and that that was a sort of massive trauma to him somehow.

This academic had presented the cartoons as a way of mapping media manipulation and Muslim leaders' reactions, and she regretted that she had upset the student. Yet this phenomenon can itself be manipulated: right-wing populist leaders tap into this sensitivity among some Muslims and use it as a justification for Islamophobia, to demand libertarian rights of free expression and to gain political traction.

Such cases involve populists hijacking human rights discourse in order to protect their own power. Bilkova (2019) demonstrates how human rights can be both appealed to by populists (insisting upon their right to speak freely) and misused (rejecting the value of human rights by accusing them of favouring minorities). Yet we are not living in the 'endtimes of human rights' as Hopgood believes (2013). Instead it is necessary to challenge continuously those who want to say what they like without any regard for others.

The conflation of the appeal to freedom of speech and possible Islamophobia to win popular support is clear in Boris Johnson's claims about Muslim women in 2018. While campaigning to become prime minister, he described Muslim women wearing the 'burka' as looking like 'bank robbers' or 'letter boxes' (Perfect, 2018). He was ordered to apologise by the Conservative Party chairman but refused, calling the order an attack on freedom of speech (Newton Dunn, 2018). Using our four approaches to freedom of speech discussed in Chapter 1 (liberal becoming libertarian and guarded liberal becoming no-platforming), we see Johnson's article as libertarian dressed up as liberal. In the article, he tempered his insulting description by also asserting that he would not stop women from wearing the 'burka'. In this way, populist politicians like Johnson achieve two aims. They signal to the public that they are unafraid to speak their mind and are defenders of freedom of speech. Simultaneously, they push public views about freedom of speech away from the liberal or guarded liberal models and towards the libertarian model, which they legitimise and exemplify.

Populist hate speech and university no-platforming

It is a commonly used right-wing libertarian device to accuse university students of being 'snowflakes' – people who melt into emotional irrationality whenever faced with opposing views – and of stifling every 'ordinary' person's right to freedom of speech, as exemplified by the claim of political journalist Fraser Nelson (2018) that 'Free speech is crumbling under the weight of the young's easy outrage'. He even accused students of taking these censorious attitudes into the workplace when they graduate, threatening the long-term health of society.

Right-wing populist leaders exploit this narrative of moral panic. When campaigning for his Brexit Party in 2019, Nigel Farage accused universities of 'constant bias, prejudice and [left-wing] brainwashing', and of fostering a culture hostile to right-leaning students:

> [L]ots of students that I've met ... say 'Nigel, we're scared to say what we think because of the abuse we'll get from professors and our fellow pupils'.
>
> (Morgan, 2019)

Claiming that key elements of liberal democracy like universities, judges and even the 'mainstream media' are all betraying the people is a crucial move used by populists to garner support. Some students respond to these narratives of moral panic by moving further towards libertarianism. In contrast, as we show in Chapter 4, more students react to extreme libertarian speech by advocating guarded liberalism or even the no-platforming approach for speech they consider offensive or racist.

In shifting towards guarded liberalism and no-platforming, many students are aligning with those theorists who advocate varying levels of censorship against right-wing populists who spread 'hate speech'. There is much disagreement about defining hate speech, including frequent attempts to explain it as objectively recognisable in any circumstance. Boromisza-Habashi (2013: 23) gives a general definition of hate speech as utterances 'directed against groups of people and arous[ing] fear in them in a strategic and conscious manner'. Even if we accept this, there is much disagreement about what to do about it and whether the context must be considered. Waldron (2012) and Parekh (2012) propose that hate speech must be legislated against. Waldron (2012: 4) uses metaphors such as 'slow-acting poison' to describe hate speech: this may be accurate, but it is also misleading in that it implies all hate speech is intrinsically poisonous.

In contrast, Heinze disagrees that hate speech (howsoever defined) should be banned. Hate speech is, Heinze admits, a blight on human relationships, but he argues it must always be understood and dealt with in the context in which it arises. This context is often a democracy, which is where hate speech must be tackled – where inequalities create the contexts that cause the hate speech (Heinze, 2016: 79). He believes that Parekh is wrong to assume a one-size-fits-all model for democracies, when in fact there are many different types, with different manifestations of freedom of speech. This means it is inappropriate to make universally applicable judgements about handling hate speech.

There are other strategies for handling hate speech than banning it, of course. Advocates of no-platforming of far-right populists as a default position, for example, correctly point out that 'Not all ideas are equal' and deserving of equal public exposure, and that it cannot be assumed that exposing such views to 'sunlight' will successfully 'disinfect' them (Mulhall, 2019).

There is considerable sympathy for such positions within Higher Education. Some students' unions have adopted 'safe space' policies. This refers to an attempt to create social and educational places in which members of minority groups can speak freely, those who normally feel silenced by imbalances of power. Meanwhile, the National Union of Students (NUS) has a policy of not inviting people from a number of organisations it considers racist or fascist (some proscribed, some not) to speak at its events (NUS, 2017).

In the *Re/presenting Islam on Campus* research project (see Chapter 4), Scott-Baumann and her team encountered the belief that no-platforming is necessary to preserve the rights and freedom of speech of minority groups. As a white male non-religious postdoctoral researcher said:

> I wouldn't defend a fascist using free speech, because their agenda means no free speech in the future. So, you think about long-term aims.

This is a utopian belief that individual acts (like no-platforming a fascist) can transform society for the better. To balance hateful ideologies we need utopia: utopian thought and language have the energy to oppose the given order and replace it with something better. This means facing up to such an ideology to dismantle it. But we must also accept that utopia can be extreme in its own way, as in this example where the student denies the right to freedom of speech to someone whose view he opposes. We may need to become more pragmatic in how we respond to hate speech from right-wing populists. Students' unions customarily avoid inviting right-wing speakers like Farage, which deprives the student community of the opportunity to challenge them and weaken their power.

We find Heinze's arguments convincing here. In a 2016 article, he presents ten arguments for no-platforming, matched by ten (stronger ones) against (Heinze, 2016). He clearly prefers a democratic position that encourages the liberal approach to freedom of speech, allowing people to speak freely within the law. He finds this preferable to a no-platforming rights-based approach that finds it very difficult to balance one person's right against that of another.

The extent of no-platforming on campus

Undoubtedly there have been some high-profile cases of students attempting to deny a platform to people they do not like. A particularly concerning case involved the former Home Secretary Amber Rudd, whose invitation to speak at the University of Oxford in 2020 was cancelled by the inviting society merely 30 minutes before the start of the event, following pressure from students (Grierson, 2020). But we cannot assume that such attempts are either common in universities or successful. Media reports about university speaker events often describe incidents as 'no-platforming' when in fact something more complex has occurred. An oft-cited example is that of the feminist Germaine Greer, who was invited to give a lecture at Cardiff University in 2015. Student activists called for her to be no-platformed for her 'transphobic' views. Instead, the university ensured the event went ahead the following month, though it issued a statement distancing itself from 'discriminatory comments' (Packham, 2016).

Regardless of student attempts at silencing, very few succeed. The vast majority of requests for events and speakers are upheld by universities. According to the Office for Students, out of 62,094 external speaker events requested in English universities in 2017–18, only 53 (0.09%) were rejected (Office for Students, 2019: 10). In 2018, the BBC Reality Check team issued Freedom of Information requests to universities and received responses from 120 of them. Since 2010 there were the following episodes: six occasions on which universities cancelled speakers as a result of complaints; seven student complaints about course content being in some way offensive or inappropriate (in four of these cases action was taken); and no instances of books being removed or banned (Schraer and Butcher, 2018). This is a tiny number of incidents and should dispel the narrative so popular with right-wing populists that freedom of speech in universities is in crisis.

But lack of a crisis in freedom of speech does not mean that there are not threats to it. The statistics cited earlier do not tell us how many requests for external speakers are discouraged informally by staff, nor the extent to which students are deciding not to make requests for the speakers they want, out of risk aversion. In the following chapters, we examine these issues in detail.

Conclusion

Populism is currently mostly right-wing. Populist leaders become influential by deploying rhetoric that sets up an 'us v them' binary, racist tactics against Muslims and migrants and Jewish people. On a few university campuses there is left-wing populism; such movements may categorically exclude all multi-viewpoint debate about certain issues like transgender rights, Israel/Palestine or the removal of statues. Right-wing populists, meanwhile, have hijacked human rights arguments. They assert their own right to speak freely in libertarian, absolutist ways while denying that right to others. Paradoxically, they also challenge the legitimacy of human rights and claim that the rights of minorities (migrants and Muslims) are unfairly privileged over those of the general population. Such debates are characterised by a lack of facts.

With regard to the ways in which human rights arguments are both misused and challenged in the freedom of speech debate, we are not arguing that the liberal elite roots of the rights discourse are poisoning the human rights tree as Hopgood proposes (2016). However, liberal democratic hopes can be distorted: right-wing populists use exaggerated versions to ask too much or too little of the rights-based discourse, which then cannot function fairly. To avoid such distortion and strengthen liberal democracy, Alston (2017: 13) echoes Laclau and Mouffe, arguing that human rights groups must work more on economic and social rights; we believe this entails closer engagement with their opponents, including authoritarian, anti-rights groups.

If we are to resist right-wing populism, it is necessary to retain one positive aspect of populism: its desire to speak truth to power. But we must also learn to overcome populism's seductive binary of 'us v them', which tempts us to view our political opponents as dehumanised enemies. The utopian mode of progress must encourage the imagination rather than merely critiquing the ideologies we seek to topple: open discussion is the first step. Democratic populism is the solution, as advocated by Laclau (2005) (with populist reason), Mouffe (2013) (with agonism), Chwalisz (2019) (with deliberative democracy) and Abou El Fadl (2001) (with Islamic pluralistic community practice). Each can help to disrupt authoritarian posturing. In Chapter 7 we show how universities can help students to do this.

Right-wing populism is also driving the freedom of speech wars on campus. Populist leaders tap into people's worries that universities are failing to uphold this freedom or are abusing it and giving Islamist extremists free rein. By pointing to both these narratives of moral panic, populist leaders are able to bolster their argument that the central institutions of liberal democracy are failing 'the people'. But these narratives are largely baseless and are also misdirected: the focus of their concern is on students, rather than on wider structures that are driving risk aversion on campus. The following chapters interrogate these in detail.

References

Abou El Fadl, K. (2001) *And God Knows the Soldiers: The Authoritative and Authoritarian in Islamic Discourses.* Lanham, MD: University Press of America.

Agamben, G. (2005) *State of Exception.* Chicago: University of Chicago Press, 2005.

Alston, P. (2017) 'The Populist Challenge to Human Rights', *Journal of Human Rights Practice*, 9, 1: 1–15. https://academic.oup.com/jhrp/article/9/1/1/3772736.

Baker, P.C. (2019) '"We the People": The Battle to Define Populism', *The Guardian*, 10 January. https://www.theguardian.com/news/2019/jan/10/we-the-people-the-battle-to-define-populism.

Bartlett, J. (2014) 'Populism, Social Media and Democratic Strain'. In Sandelind, C. (ed.) *European Populism and Winning the Immigration Debate*. Stockholm: Fores: 99–116.

Bilkova, V. (2019) 'Populism and Human Rights'. In Nijman, J. and Werner, W. (eds.) *Netherlands Yearbook of International Law*, vol. 49. The Hague: T.M.C. Asser Press: 143–174. https://link.springer.com/chapter/10.1007/978-94-6265-331-3_7.

Booth, J. and Baert, P. (2018) *The Dark Side of Podemos?: Carl Schmitt and Contemporary Progressive Populism*. London: Routledge.

Boromisza-Habashi, D. (2013) *Speaking Hatefully*. Philadelphia: Penn State University Press.

Burman, J. (2015) 'Nigel Farage Warns Turkey Joining EU Could EXPOSE Bloc to Evil ISIS Terrorists', *The Express*, 3 December. https://www.express.co.uk/news/uk/623849/UKIP-Nigel-Farage-Turkey-European-Union-Brussels-Ankara-Islamic-State-Migration-ISIS-Daesh.

Butler, J. (2015) *Notes Towards a Performative Theory of Assembly*. Cambridge, MA: Harvard University Press.

Chwalisz, C. (2019) 'A New Wave of Deliberative Democracy', *Carnegie Europe*, 26 November. https://carnegieeurope.eu/2019/11/26/new-wave-of-deliberative-democracy-pub-80422.

Ebner, J. (2020) *Going Dark: The Secret Social Lives of Extremists*. London: Bloomsbury.

Frankfurt, H. (1986) 'On Bullshit', *Raritan* 6, 2: 81–100. http://www2.csudh.edu/ccauthen/576f12/frankfurt__harry_-_on_bullshit.pdf.

Garikipati, S. and Kambhampati, U. (2020) 'Leading the Fight Against the Pandemic: Does Gender 'Really' Matter?', *SSRN*: 1–16. http://dx.doi.org/10.2139/ssrn.3617953.

Green, A. (2019) 'Speaking Bullshit to Power: Populism and the Rhetoric of Bullshit'. https://papers.ssrn.com/sol3/papers.cfm?abstract_id=3382161.

Grierson, J. (2020) 'Amber Rudd Hits out at "Rude" Oxford Students after Talk Cancelled', *The Guardian*, 6 March. https://www.theguardian.com/politics/2020/mar/06/amber-rudd-hits-out-at-rude-oxford-students-after-talk-cancelled.

Hawkins, K.A., Carlin, R.E., Littvay, L. and Rovira Kaltwasser, C. (eds.) (2019) *The Ideational Approach to Populism? Concept, Theory, and Analysis*. London: Routledge.

Heinze, E. (2016) 'Ten Arguments for – And Against – "No-Platforming"', *Free Speech Debate*, 1 March. https://freespeechdebate.com/en/discuss/ten-arguments-for-and-against-no-platforming/

Hopgood, S. (2013) *The Endtimes of Human Rights*. Ithaca, NY: Cornell University Press.
Hopgood, S. (2016) 'Fascism Rising', *Open Democracy*, 9 November. https://www.opendemocracy.net/en/openglobalrights-openpage/fascism-rising/.
KhosraviNik, M. and Unger, J.W. (2016) 'Critical Discourse Studies and Social Media: Power, Resistance and Critique in Changing Media Ecologies'. In Wodak, R. and Meyer, M. (eds.) *Methods of Critical Discourse Studies*. 3rd ed. London: Sage: 205–234.
Kumar, A. (2014) 'Looking Back at Obama's Campaign in 2008: 'True Blue Populist' and Social Production of Empty Signifiers in Political Reporting', *Journal of Communication Inquiry*, 38, 1: 5–24. https://journals.sagepub.com/doi/abs/10.1177/0196859913512330.
Laclau, E. (2005) *On Populist Reason*. London: Verso.
Leone, G. (2013) 'Sometimes I, Sometimes Me: A Study on the Use of Autobiographical Memories in Two Political Speeches by Barack Obama'. In Poggi, I., D'Errico, F., Vincze, L., and Vinciarelli, A. (eds.) *Multimodal Communication in Political Speech. Shaping Minds and Social Action*. Dordrecht: Springer: 133–148.
Leone, G., di Murro, F. and Serlupi Crescenzi, L. (2015). 'From Personalization to Parrhesia: A Multimodal Analysis of Autobiographical Recalls in Barack Obama's Political Speech'. In d'Errico, F., Poggi, I., Vinciarelli, A. and Vincze, L. (eds.) *Conflict and Multimodal Communication. Social Research and Machine Intelligence*. Berlin: Springer: 349–374.
Minogue, K. (1969) 'Populism as a Political Movement'. In Ionescu, G. and Gellner, E., (eds.) *Populism: Its Meaning and National Characteristics*. New York: Macmillan: 197–211.
Morgan, J. (2019) 'Universities in Firing Line as Farage Builds Populist Movement', *Times Higher Education*, 29 May. https://www.timeshighereducation.com/news/universities-firing-line-farage-builds-populist-movement.
Mouffe, C. (2013) *Agonistics: Thinking the World Politically*. London: Verso.
Mouffe, C. (2014) 'Democracy, Human Rights and Cosmopolitanism: An Agonistic Approach'. In Douzinas, C. and Gearty, C. (eds.) *The Meaning of Rights: The Philosophy and Social Theory of Human Rights*. Cambridge: Cambridge University Press: 181–192.
Mudde, C. and Rovira Kaltwasser, C. (2017) *Populism: A Very Short Introduction*. Oxford: Oxford University Press.
Mulhall, J. (2019) 'Deplatforming Works: Let's Get on with It', *HOPE not hate*, 4 October. https://www.hopenothate.org.uk/2019/10/04/deplatforming-works-lets-get-on-with-it/.
Müller, J.-W. (2016) *What Is Populism?* Philadelphia: University of Pennsylvania Press.
Myerson, G. (2001) *Heidegger, Habermas and the Mobile Phone*. London: Icon.
Myre, G. (2019) 'From Threats against Salman Rushdie to Attacks on "Charlie Hebdo"', *NPR*, 8 January. https://www.npr.org/sections/parallels/

2015/01/08/375662895/from-threats-against-salman-rushdie-to-attacks-on-charlie-hebdo?t=1565731350344&t=1593240687492.

National Union of Students (NUS) (2017) *NUS' No Platform Policies*. https://www.nusconnect.org.uk/resources/nus-no-platform-policy-f22f.

Nelson, F. (2018) 'Free Speech Is Crumbling under the Weight of the Young's Easy Outrage', *The Telegraph*, 5 October. https://www.telegraph.co.uk/news/2018/10/05/free-speech-crumbling-weight-youngs-easy-outrage/.

Newton Dunn, T. (2018) 'Boris Johnson Blasts "Attack on Free Speech" as Theresa May and Top Tories Demand Apology over Burka Jibe', *The Sun*, 7 August. https://www.thesun.co.uk/news/6964104/boris-johnson-theresa-may-apologise-burka-comment/.

Office for Students (2019) *Prevent Monitoring Accountability and Data Returns 2017–18: Evaluation Report*. London: Office for Students. https://www.officeforstudents.org.uk/media/860e26e2-63e7-47eb-84e0-49100788009c/ofs2019_22.pdf.

Packham, A. (2016) 'Boris, Tatchell, Greer: Were They Actually No-Platformed?', *The Guardian*, 5 May. https://www.theguardian.com/education/2016/may/05/boris-tatchell-greer-were-they-actually-no-platformed.

Pajnik, M. and Sauer, B. (2019) *Populism and the Web*. London: Routledge.

Parekh, B. (2012) 'Is There a Case for Banning Hate Speech?' In Herz, M. and Molnar, P. (eds.) *The Content and Context of Hate Speech: Rethinking Regulation and Responses*. Cambridge: Cambridge University Press: 37–56.

Perfect, S. (2018) 'Boris and His Burka: Criticising His Language Is Not Restricting Free Speech', *Theos*, 9 August. https://www.theosthinktank.co.uk/comment/2018/08/09/boris-and-his-burka-criticising-his-language-is-not-restricting-free-speech.

Pohjonen, M. (2018) *Horizons of Hate: A Comparative Approach to Social Media Hate Speech*. VOX-Pol Network of Excellence. https://www.voxpol.eu/download/vox-pol_publication/Horizons-of-Hate.pdf.

PoliticsHome (2019) 'Boris Johnson's First Speech as Prime Minister', *PoliticsHome*, 24 July. https://www.politicshome.com/news/article/read-in-full-boris-johnsons-first-speech-as-prime-minister.

Ricoeur, P. (1976) 'Ideology and Utopia as Cultural Imagination', *Philosophic Exchange*, 7, 1: 16–28. http://digitalcommons.brockport.edu/phil_ex/vol7/iss1/5.

Schmitt, C. (1988) *The Crisis of Parliamentary Democracy*. Translated by E. Kennedy. Boston, MA: MIT Press. First published in 1923.

Schraer, R. and Butcher, B. (2018) 'Universities: Is Free Speech under Threat?' *The Telegraph*, 23 October. https://www.bbc.co.uk/news/education-45447938.

Scott-Baumann, A. (2013) *Ricoeur and the Negation of Happiness*. London: Bloomsbury.

Scott-Baumann, A. (2017) 'Ideology, Utopia and Islam on Campus: How to Free Speech a Little from Its Own Terrors', *Education, Citizenship and Social Justice*, 12, 2: 159–176. https://journals.sagepub.com/toc/esja/12/2.

Waldron, J. (2012) *The Harm in Hate Speech*. Cambridge, MA: Harvard University Press.

3 The Prevent Duty and the views of university Prevent Leads

The year 2015 was a key moment for universities, and for Muslim students and staff in particular: the passing of the Counter-Terrorism and Security Act (CTSA) and (in England, Wales and Scotland) the introduction of the Prevent Duty. Section 26.1 of the CTSA places a legal duty on public institutions to:

> [H]ave due regard to the need to prevent people from being drawn into terrorism.

Universities and other institutions are required to train staff to identify people potentially being radicalised into terrorism and refer them to the authorities. This Duty is a sub-branch of the Prevent strategy – the programme to stop people from becoming terrorists or supporting terrorism (Home Office, 2011a) – which itself is one of the four strands of CONTEST, the UK's strategy for countering terrorism, established in 2003 after 9/11. Of the four strands, Prevent has received the most public attention and criticism, not least because it has faced repeated accusations of unfairly targeting and stigmatising Muslims.

In this chapter, we survey the development of Prevent, before examining the government's Prevent Duty Guidance for Higher Education. This guidance has been highly controversial, particularly in relation to freedom of speech for external speakers. We examine a range of criticisms that have been levelled at Prevent. Useful here are Kant's injunction that we should be able to turn every moral judgement into a rule that is applicable to all, Strauss's 'persuasion principle', and our consideration of the decisionist nature of right-wing politics (Schmitt).

We also summarise findings from our research (conducted from 2017 to 2019) with eight university managers responsible for implementing the Prevent Duty in their institutions ('Prevent Leads'). These are important players in the Prevent debate who are often overlooked.

We explore their different approaches to implementation, the challenges they face, and their perceptions of Prevent's impact on freedom of speech and Muslims.

This chapter also highlights the lack of clarity about many of the concepts in this discussion, including 'extremism' and 'radicalisation'. Even 'terrorism' is an ambiguous term because in UK legislation it applies not only to violent actions that seek to advance some ideological cause, but also to non-violent acts such as inviting support for a proscribed organisation and viewing or possessing material (online or offline) useful for terrorists (Terrorism Act 2000: s. 1) (Counter-Terrorism and Border Security Act 2019: s. 1–3).

The development of Prevent

Prevent is concerned with 'pre-crime' – with changing people's ideas *before* they become radicalised into terrorism. It is underpinned by a particular way of thinking about terrorism, which sees beliefs and ideologies (particularly religious and usually Islamic ones) as the main cause of terrorist violence (Heath-Kelly, 2017). Practically, it involves structures to identify people thought to be vulnerable to radicalisation into extreme views and techniques intended to deconstruct those views (Holmwood and O'Toole, 2017).

Publicly launched in 2006, following the 7/7 bombings, Prevent was initially administered by the Department of Communities and Local Government (DCLG) and focused explicitly and primarily on Muslims. In part, this involved funding community-based organisations, specifically in areas with high levels of Muslims, to deter people from 'Islamist extremism' (Home Office, 2006; Thomas, 2014). The government also funded national-level initiatives. These included programmes to raise standards in mosques, through partnership with the Mosques and Imams National Advisory Board (MINAB), and projects such as the Radical Middle Way to promote 'mainstream Islamic scholars' to challenge extreme interpretations of Islam (Home Office, 2009: 82–95). Muslim women, often imagined as oppressed by their communities, were seen as 'moderate' bulwarks against extremism, so the government funded initiatives to empower them (Rashid, 2016).

Prevent was revised substantially in 2011 following mounting criticism, including from Parliament's Communities and Local Government Committee (2010). Responsibilities for promoting integration and preventing terrorism, which previously had gone together, were separated, with the DCLG managing the former and the Home Office the latter.

Prevent became increasingly centralised, with local authorities having less control (Heath-Kelly, 2017: 301). The Coalition government argued that previous Prevent funding had gone to Muslim organisations that supported extremism; from now on, only groups deemed to be fully opposed to extremism would be supported (Home Office, 2011b: 34–35).

The 2011 iteration of Prevent also broadened from the previous focus on 'violent' extremism to incorporate 'non-violent' forms (Home Office, 2011b: 6). The 2011 strategy defined extremism as:

> [V]ocal or active opposition to fundamental British values, including democracy, the rule of law, individual liberty and mutual respect and tolerance of different faiths and beliefs.
> (Home Office, 2011b: 107)

In 2014 the government issued guidance for schools about embedding these values into curricula (Department for Education, 2014). These binary conceptions of 'extremism' and 'British values', and their connection to terrorism, have been criticised for their ambiguity and subjectivity. These criticisms increased after the passing of the CTSA in 2015 (see following), and the difficulty of defining 'extremism' in law led to the failure of the May government's attempt to pass a Counter-Extremism Bill (Townsend, 2017).

The Channel programme, which was rolled out across England and Wales in 2012, is a key part of the counter-terrorism infrastructure (in Scotland it is known as Prevent Professional Concerns [PPC]). Individuals identified as potentially being drawn into terrorism are referred to a Prevent officer (in the police or local authority) for screening, before being referred to the Channel/PPC programmes. These local, multi-agency panels evaluate each case and develop a support package. Individuals assessed as posing a terrorism threat might be offered personal coaching, including Home Office-approved theological mentoring (Home Office, 2015b: 10–13; 17). Participation in the Channel support package is voluntary, but people raising a 'Prevent concern' are not required to secure the individual's consent (or inform them) before making a referral (Home Office, 2015b: 16; Home Office, n.d.a). Details of everyone referred to Prevent are maintained on a national police database. Concerns have been expressed about how such data might affect the individuals (most of whom have not committed an offence) later in life, although the government insists that Prevent referrals do not result in a criminal record (Grierson, 2019b; Home Office, 2019b: 3).

The year 2018 saw another revision of CONTEST in response to the 2017 terrorist attacks in Britain, seeking to address the potential emerging threats posed by British ISIS jihadists returning from overseas and by far-right extremists. This iteration emphasises the importance of removing online extremist-related content and promoting 'counter-narrative[s]' (Home Office, 2018: 34–35; 92). It also attempts to move away from the previous focus on ideology as driving radicalisation, instead emphasising multiple factors, and acknowledges that: 'Few of those who are drawn into terrorism have a deep knowledge of faith' (Home Office, 2018: 32). This marks a considerable shift from the original CONTEST's focus on a 'distorted form of Islam' as the primary driver (Home Office, 2006: 7). How far this theoretical shift has been reflected in practice, however, is unclear.

Finally, in 2019 a Commission for Countering Extremism reviewed the current strategy. Led by Sara Khan (known for her counter-extremism work with the government and support of Prevent), it proposed a concept of 'hateful extremism' – behaviours that incite hatred and cause harm. It emphasised the distinction between radicalisation into terrorism and extremism, arguing that counter-terrorism and counter-extremism work have tended to overlap unhelpfully (Commission for Countering Extremism, 2019: 5–12; 79). In 2020 Khan launched a review of existing legislation, noting that extremists are able to propagate hateful material that does not meet the threshold of terrorism (Commission for Countering Extremism, 2020). Further legal bans on hate speech would be supported by Waldron (2012), but we argue that any proposed changes must not undermine people's ability to criticise the beliefs of others.

The Prevent Duty in universities: Pushing guarded liberalism and no-platforming

For universities, the most important development has been the CTSA and the Prevent Duty's introduction in 2015. This massively expanded and de-professionalised counter-terror work, putting it into the hands of non-specialist public-sector workers. This co-opting of public institutions completed Prevent's transformation from being administered in particular regions to being administered across the population (Heath-Kelly, 2017: 301; O'Toole et al., 2016).

Cameron's government considered education institutions as particularly vulnerable to extremism and external speakers invited onto campus as a key way of spreading it. Indeed, when the Duty was introduced, a Downing Street press release specifically addressed the Further and Higher Education sectors (implying extremism was widespread there), claiming that in the previous year universities hosted over 70 events involving speakers 'known to have promoted rhetoric that aimed to undermine core British values' (Department for Business, Innovation and Skills et al., 2015). The wording closely paraphrased a report by Student Rights, a project of the neoconservative think tank the Henry Jackson Society, which is important for shaping government assumptions about extremism (see Chapter 4) (Grove, 2015; Sutton, 2015: 12–14).

The Prevent Duty obliges universities to curb the expression of views that may lead people to terrorism. Thus it conflicts with universities' duty, under the Education (No. 2) Act 1986, to uphold freedom of speech as far as possible within the law. This tension is even present within the CTSA itself – Section 31 requires universities to have a 'particular regard' to 'the duty to ensure freedom of speech', and to 'the importance of academic freedom' when fulfilling Prevent (Counter-Terrorism and Security Act 2015: s. 31).

Government guidance on implementing the Duty in universities, known as the Prevent Duty Guidance (Home Office, 2015a), exacerbated this tension between competing legal duties. The Duty expects universities to assess the risks associated with any events and to ensure that 'extremist' speakers are challenged by someone with 'opposing views', to achieve balance (Home Office, 2019a: paras 11–12). This guidance has been highly controversial, particularly because Paragraph 11 requires universities to cancel events if they cannot '*fully* mitigate' (emphasis added) the risk that any views likely to be expressed 'constitute extremist views that risk drawing people into terrorism or are shared by terrorist groups' (Home Office, 2019a: para 11; Scott-Baumann and Tomlinson, 2016). The Joint Committee on Human Rights (JCHR) and Universities UK criticised this wording because it is impossible to 'fully mitigate' any risk (JCHR, 2018: 30; Universities UK, 2018). Moreover, it has been argued (for example, by Helen Mountfield QC, a human rights lawyer) that the guidance encourages universities to have an 'overanxious approach' to stopping controversial, though lawful, speech, which conflicts with their freedom of speech duty (JCHR, 2017: 6).

The guidance's status was tested in a judicial review on behalf of Dr Salman Butt – the chief editor of islam21c.com, who was named in the 2015 Downing Street press release as an extremist who had spoken at universities (Department for Business, Innovation and Skills et al., 2015). In 2019, in the Butt case, the Court of Appeal found Paragraph 11 of the guidance to be misleading and unlawful because it is likely to push universities to disregard their legal duty to uphold external speakers' freedom of speech (*R (on the application of Salman Butt) v*

The Secretary of the State for the Home Department. [2019], paras 176–177). In other words, the guidance pushes universities towards risk aversion and the guarded liberal or even no-platforming approaches to freedom of speech as a default position, for speakers with lawful, though controversial, views. This exacerbates other factors pushing universities towards risk aversion, including the actions of lobbying groups that pressurise universities into cancelling events by threatening disruption.

The courts clarified that the guidance is only relevant to extremism that risks drawing people into *terrorism*, not all extremism, and that while universities must *consider* the guidance, they are not required to follow it to any particular outcome (such as cancelling events). They can decide that their duty to have 'particular regard' for freedom of speech is 'more important' than their duty to have 'due regard' to stop people from being drawn into terrorism (*Salman Butt v The Secretary of the State for the Home Department.* [2017] paras 30, 61–62, 98).

This guidance still governs Prevent in universities, and as of summer 2020, the government has not revised it. Despite the legal clarifications, many universities presumably still follow its risk-averse logic, erroneously thinking that to comply with Prevent they must restrict (guarded liberalism) or even prevent (no-platforming) speech from people with extreme or controversial views. Guarded liberal measures that restrict free speech (such as requiring speakers to submit speeches in advance for vetting) are not necessarily problematic and may sometimes be the most appropriate way to handle very controversial high-profile speakers. However, when a university *regularly* imposes these conditions as its standard response to speakers with controversial views, or who are speaking about divisive topics, it creates a culture of risk aversion, which in turn can deter students from requesting such speakers or debates in the first place.

This also affects students' unions. The Prevent Duty does not apply directly to the unions, which are legal entities distinct from their parent universities. However, each union is required to comply with its university's code of practice on free speech, which will usually incorporate Prevent's concerns about extremism and speaker events.

Conceptual problems with Prevent

Prevent has faced considerable criticism since 2006, including accusations of Islamophobia (Muslim Council of Britain, 2019) and of stigmatising Muslims (see following). The JCHR has challenged the vagueness of the definition of 'extremism' and Prevent's apparent reliance on a 'conveyor belt' theory of radicalisation, which sees religious conservatism as leading inexorably towards extremism and terrorism (JCHR, 2016: 24–29; Qurashi, 2017: 205). While recent government documents emphasise there is 'no single pathway' leading someone into terrorism (Home Office, 2018: 32), in practice referrals to Prevent continue to be made primarily, and unwarrantedly, from concerns about individuals' perceived religious conservatism – including in universities. It is worth noting that among academic specialists, there is no consensus on the importance of beliefs and ideologies as opposed to other factors such as socio-economic issues in the process(es) of radicalisation. As Hardy shows, the UK's tendency to give primacy to ideology in its counter-terrorism strategy is not the only approach, and other countries do differently (Hardy, 2018: 82–90, 96–98).

Others have challenged the credibility of research underpinning Prevent, particularly regarding the 'signs' of radicalisation. In England and Wales, people referred to Channel are assessed against 22 factors (the Extremism Risk Guidance (ERG) 22+), to determine whether they are being radicalised into terrorism. These include a sense of 'grievance'; a desire for 'identity, meaning and belonging'; '"Them" and Us" thinking'; and having the intention and capacity to cause harm (Home Office, 2012: 2–3).[1] The factors derive from a small psychological study of convicted prisoners affiliated to Islam, some but not all of whom had sought to commit terrorism (National Offender Management Service, 2011). The study remains classified, so its methodology cannot be scrutinised properly by other psychologists (though the authors have published summary articles – see Dean, 2014; Lloyd and Dean, 2015; Lloyd, 2016). Various academics and organisations, including the Royal College of Psychiatrists, have criticised the government's worrying lack of transparency here (Qureshi, 2016: 4; 7; Ross, 2016; Royal College of Psychiatrists, 2016; Scarcella et al., 2016). As for the ERG22+ itself, in 2019 Ministry of Justice researchers tested it against 171 people convicted of unspecified Islamist extremism-related offences. They considered it useful for identifying the risk posed by such offenders but identified some limitations. They also made clear that ERG22+ is intended for use by 'qualified forensic professionals' with people who have *already* been convicted of an 'any extremist or extremist-related offence' (Powis et al., 2019: 5). Therefore it is unclear how appropriate it is for use by non-psychologists in the Channel process.

Here it is worth pausing to consider what the Prevent Duty means to achieve. Behavioural psychologist B.F. Skinner demonstrated that paying attention to a person's behaviour will increase the likelihood of them repeating it. This association between behaviour and response can be used to reinforce good or bad behaviour. One can encourage desirable behaviours in others by focusing on and discussing them; conversely, you should ignore behaviours you do not want repeated (Skinner, 1988; Scott-Baumann et al., 2000: 49–54). This forms the basis of much childrearing and pedagogy. Prevent functions against the grain of this, instead paying attention to behaviours it seeks to eliminate (negative reinforcement). Moreover, arguably it exacerbates wider societal pressure on Muslims to 'secularise' and avoid external signs of religiosity, by encouraging those tasked with spotting radicalisation to pay attention to such signs (see following). But this pressure may actually lead to some Muslims deepening their faith and religious practices.

Most importantly, there is little evidence that radicalisation into terrorism is actually a major issue in our universities. In the 1990s and 2000s, the government was concerned that Islamist groups like Hizb ut-Tahrir were infiltrating campuses (Home Office, 2011b: 73), but only a very small number of people seem to have joined or engaged in terrorist causes while studying at university. In 2019, for example, a captured jihadist revealed he was one of several students and ex-students from the same London university to have joined ISIS (Swann et al., 2019). Yet for the small number of ex-student jihadists, it is not possible to prove they were radicalised while studying. The Henry Jackson Society conducted a study of all 253 people convicted in the United Kingdom for an Islamist-related terrorist offence between 1998 and 2015; only 13 of them (4.8%) were in Higher Education at the time of their arrest, and only 3 (1.1%) had recently left full-time education (Stuart, 2017: 942 Table 8). Similarly, a BBC database of 276 known British jihadists lists only 13 (4.7%) as university students. Seven were not even members of British institutions, but were studying in Khartoum (BBC News, 2017).

Data from the Office for Students (OfS) show that the number of referrals made to Channel by English universities is tiny – a mere 15 referrals were made in 2017–18 (OfS, 2019: 10). These figures support the Home Affairs Committee in its 2012 review of Prevent, which concluded that 'there is seldom concrete evidence' that universities are sites of radicalisation, and the emphasis placed on universities by the government 'is now disproportionate' (House of Commons Home Affairs Committee, 2012: 18).

These facts also challenge the government's identification of university external speakers as posing a particular threat – a flawed assumption considering the lack of evidence that attending one-off events with 'extreme' speakers makes students more likely to commit terrorism. The logic here is that extreme ideas are contagious like a virus, and that students are vulnerable to them by being in proximity to an extreme speaker. This assumes that students are passive agents vulnerable to being infected at university events, lacking the ability to critique ideas presented to them (Qurashi, 2017: 203–204).

If this were so, which is not proven, then it would be sensible to teach *more* about Islam rather than inhibiting coverage thereof. Indeed, Abou El Fadl proposes that *if* this were the case, it can be resolved through classroom education: by delegitimising a single authoritarian interpretation of Islam and replacing it with expert teaching, with a range of pluralist understandings (Slater, 2018: 96–97).

Prevent's focus on Muslims

Our main concern is Prevent's impact on Muslims. Prevent's critics argue that it unfairly and disproportionately targets Muslims. In the health sector, for example, a report by global health charity Medact argued that the duty on healthcare workers to spot radicalisation 'causes discrimination against Muslims and Asian communities' and damages the presumption of confidential medical care (Aked, 2020: 7). In the university sector, critics argue it has led to some Muslim students self-censoring, or avoiding requesting controversial speakers, for fear this might invite suspicion that they are extremists (JCHR, 2018: 31–32). In Chapter 4, we examine the evidence for this.

It is important to note that despite the agitation of Muslim organisations against Prevent, only 44% of Muslims have heard of it, according to a nationally representative survey of 1,000 Muslims from 2019. This is more, though, than the equivalent figure (32%) for the general public (Clements et al., 2020: 80). Thus the strength of Muslim feeling about Prevent should not be overstated. Nonetheless, we must still take very seriously the concerns of the minority of Muslims who feel stigmatised by it. Moreover, Muslims' lack of awareness of Prevent does not mean they have been unaffected by it – particularly by its impact on how others perceive them.

The Prevent Duty places (often poorly trained) non-specialist public-sector workers rather than law enforcement officers at the forefront of spotting people who are being radicalised. Relying on non-specialists (some of whom will have misconceptions about Islam and religious conservatism) inevitably leads to inappropriate referrals to Prevent. In fact, only a small proportion of people referred to Prevent are ultimately deemed to need deradicalisation support: between April 2018 and March 2019, for example, only 561 out of 5,738 Prevent referrals in England and Wales were taken forward as cases for Channel (Home Office, 2019b: 6). Since Prevent's introduction, 'Islamist extremism' accounts for the large majority of referrals to Channel (though the proportion of referrals for far-right extremism has risen in recent years); thus most of the inappropriate referrals have been Muslims (Home Office, 2019b: 10). Many of these people will feel misjudged by those around them. The long-term psychological impact of inappropriate referrals should not be underestimated, particularly because most people referred to Prevent are children – 58% of those referred in 2018–19 were under 20, and over 500 of those referred in 2015–18 were under age six (Home Office, 2019b: 9; Greenwood et al., 2020). The Medact report found that Prevent referrals in the health sector can damage people's physical and mental health, for example, by exacerbating mental health problems or by causing patients to disengage from health services (Aked, 2020: 8).

Some defenders of Prevent are unconcerned about the scale of inappropriate referrals (Greer and Bell, 2018: 95). It is possible to argue that Prevent is working as a general structure to capture all safeguarding issues. Clearly it is desirable to have structures where personal problems such as mental health issues can be identified. However, it is doubtful whether encouraging the use of Prevent as a catchall safeguarding structure is appropriate, considering its association with terrorism.

Prevent training packages

These problems are compounded by Prevent training packages, some of which encourage participants to see often ordinary behaviours as potential signs of radicalisation. For example, the Home Office's online Prevent Referral training asks participants to decide whether a vulnerable individual should be referred to Prevent under five scenarios. Four of these relate to Islamist-related extremism and only one to far-right extremism – an unfortunate set-up that may confirm some users' misconceptions about Muslims and terrorism (Home Office, n.d.b; see also Spiller et al., 2018: 130–131). One scenario is about 'Ilia', a British South Asian Muslim university student, and contains an example of a completed form referring her to Prevent, highlighting causes for concern. These include that she complained when the university cancelled an event with a potentially extreme speaker; that her standards of 'appearance' and 'demeanour' have declined; and that she has started living in a religious commune. She is also said to be confrontational, quick to anger and becoming socially isolated. Strikingly, there is no indication that Ilia has expressed extreme views or supported violence. Some listed behaviours are not unusual for stressed students, and it is unclear why her complaint in defence of the speaker's free speech, and her joining a religious commune, are potential signs of radicalisation. Nonetheless, the participant is expected to refer her to Prevent. From this scenario, participants might assume that religious change or the expression of controversial, lawful views among Muslims are to be viewed as potential signs of radicalisation (Home Office, n.d.c). This is particularly likely to affect hijab-wearing Muslim women, who are often more 'visibly Muslim' than men.

In Kantian terms, the training material's primary focus on Muslims, and its possible effect of encouraging people to treat Muslims differently from others, would be deemed immoral; it appears to violate the categorical imperative that one should only follow rules that could apply to everyone without contradiction. Finally, as this case study shows, the Home Office considers that Prevent referrals should not be limited to cases where there are signs of support for extremism. Prevent is presented as having a very broad safeguarding remit, going beyond its conception in statute as a counter-terrorism measure.

Prevent Duty 'Leads' and their perceptions of Prevent

This outline of the Prevent Duty brings us to its practical implementation in universities and the perceptions of those with responsibility for it. In their study of the views of lecturers (those on the 'front-line' of radicalisation-spotting), Spiller et al. (2018) found that their interviewees saw Prevent negatively, as threatening freedom of speech and academic freedom, and breaking down trust between them and students (especially Muslims). Some resisted Prevent by doing as little as they could to comply with it. In contrast, the interviewees perceived their university management as responding to Prevent with compliance and 'bureaucratic conservatism', wherein they sought to avoid 'controversial' events that might lead to adverse publicity. One lecturer said her university cancelled her planned terrorism conference because the speakers and topic were 'too sensitive' (Spiller et al., 2018: 140). Spiller et al. argue this risk aversion (characteristic of guarded liberalism and no-platforming) on the part of senior management creates a ripple effect, where students and staff 'restrict their expectations and behaviours' and avoid debating controversial topics (Spiller et al., 2018: 135–136).

To interrogate senior management positions further, in the following sections we explore findings from our in-depth interviews with eight Prevent Leads, conducted between late 2017 and early 2019. Some were concerned primarily with Islamist extremism; others viewed far-right extremism as a higher risk. Some had had incidents where students tried (with mixed success) to join armed groups in Syria; these had shaped the debate about Prevent on their campus (such as by dampening down student opposition to it). The universities were chosen to reflect the sector's diversity, broadly following Guest et al.'s (2013) typology of UK universities and including both urban and rural campuses. We consider the Prevent Leads' approaches to implementing the Duty, the challenges they faced in doing so, and their views on its impact on freedom of speech and Muslims.

Implementing the Prevent Duty

Universities vary greatly in their approaches to implementing Prevent. Some of our interviewees made Prevent training mandatory for all student-facing staff. In stark contrast, one Scottish university decided to train only 15–20 senior staff and to ensure that information on the Duty was available to others. The Prevent Lead considered this a 'proportionate response to the risk the university faces'. Scottish universities are regulated differently from English universities and have had more freedom to adopt a light-touch approach to implementation.[2]

One interviewee suggested that universities adopt either a 'securitised' or a 'safeguarding, pastoral' approach to Prevent. This determines how far responsibility for Prevent lies with security or pastoral staff and how far students at risk of radicalisation are seen as a security threat, or victims in need of support. In general, our interviewees described their approach as safeguarding. They encouraged staff to treat concerns about student radicalisation in the same way as other concerns such as drug abuse – as something to be passed to the safeguarding team, which would determine whether a referral to Prevent was necessary. This understanding reflects the Home Office's conception of Prevent. It is not without criticism, however. As Qurashi argues, imagining radicalisation as no different from domestic violence or child abuse obscures the rational agency of those involved and sidelines the need to discuss political injustices, which may be factors driving people towards dissent (O'Donnell, 2016: 62; Qurashi, 2017: 204).

Our interviewees differed in their willingness to embed Prevent into existing safeguarding policies. Some did this thoroughly, while others preferred to adopt a stand-alone Prevent policy. Sometimes this was due to the senior management's own scepticism about Prevent and their unwillingness to embed it too deeply (and irreversibly).

Prevent Leads also differ in how wide they think the Duty's remit should be. In one London university, a staff member referred to the internal Prevent team a student who had been making far-right statements. The Prevent Lead argued that this was not a relevant issue because the Duty is strictly 'about are they being drawn into terrorism'. She did not think that other extreme or racist statements, though unpleasant, should be flagged to the Prevent team. In sharp contrast, the Prevent Lead in a rural Welsh university understood the Duty as being part of the university's wider pastoral strategy and as a means to challenge offensive speech and promote a culture of respect.

Challenges with implementation

Prevent Leads face various challenges when implementing the Duty, including opposition from staff and students concerned about Prevent's impact on freedom of speech and Muslims. Some interviewees were sympathetic to these concerns, while others rejected them:

> There is a perception among some students that this is about monitoring and spying on students. And that couldn't be further from the truth, in my experience.

Notably, by 2018, most interviewees felt that the strength of staff opposition to the Duty had weakened since 2015.

Our interviewees expressed dissatisfaction with the various Prevent training available, including materials produced by the Home Office and by private providers (Morey and Alibhai-Brown, 2016: 6). One Prevent Lead said that his Scottish university initially utilised the Home Office's face-to-face Workshop to Raise Awareness of Prevent (WRAP) training but found this unhelpful. The training involved videos that highlighted challenging 'orthodox' opinions as both normal and a possible sign of radicalisation – a message his staff rightly criticised as inappropriate for universities.

Strikingly, despite having to manage compliance with it, some Prevent Leads doubted Prevent's necessity or effectiveness at preventing terrorism. One Prevent Lead in a London university said the Duty added little to their existing safeguarding capacity, calling it 'a sledgehammer to crack a nut'. She doubted the resources spent on ensuring compliance with the Duty (including training hundreds of staff) was commensurate to the level of risk. Indeed, our interviewees said they had very rarely referred anyone to Prevent, and the few people who were referred tended to be deemed unsuitable for consideration at the Channel panel (meaning they were not, after all, being radicalised into terrorism). This is confirmed by the OfS data: 15 referrals made to Channel across England in 2017–18 (OfS, 2019: 10).

Freedom of speech and the impact on Muslims

Our interviewees generally thought their own approach to Prevent compliance was working well, regardless of whether they viewed it as necessary. They presented their universities as seeking to uphold the liberal approach to freedom of speech and did not think that freedom was detrimentally affected by Prevent in their own institution (though some worried about its impact elsewhere). Most also emphasised that their university management had never turned away requested external speakers. One interviewee from a university in the Northwest, who strongly supported the Duty, argued that any inhibiting factor on speech in his university came from the students' union enforcing its safe space policy overzealously, not from the Prevent Duty.

In contrast to the lecturers interviewed by Spiller et al. (2018), most of our Prevent Leads doubted that Prevent was negatively affecting the free speech of Muslims on their campus. One interviewee, from a university taking a rigorous approach to the Duty, thought that Muslim students were largely supportive:

> The Muslim students don't have a problem with it. It's more other people advocating on their behalf or for their own particular political agendas.

Where differences in attitudes arise between lecturers (Spiller et al., 2018) and managerial staff in our sample, this may reflect their different roles. The former have more direct contact with Muslim students, while the latter need to ensure the university complies with the law; this focus on compliance may mean managers are more likely to view Prevent positively or with indifference.

Another interviewee thought that talk of Prevent creating a 'chilling effect' on freedom of speech was more of a popular narrative than grounded in fact. Yet he suggested that *if* free speech was being dampened anywhere on campus, it was most likely to be among Muslims – 'They could be quite intimidated by this'.

Some of the interviewees did express concerns about the wider consequences of Prevent for Muslims. One Prevent Lead, from a London university, thought that the Prevent Duty coordinators in the local council were especially, and unfairly, focused on Muslim speakers hosted by the university:

> [We] have had some very difficult ... high profile protests on campus around left-wing speakers, and nobody has ever picked up the phone and checked with me, 'what are our regulations and how did we safeguard people in that instance?' It has only been when it is around Islamic speakers, and that is why I feel really conflicted.

Even in universities where most staff were expected to complete some form of Prevent training, problematic referrals of students to the internal Prevent team still occurred. In one case, following the London Bridge attack in 2017, an academic in a London university informed senior staff about a Muslim student who the academic thought was becoming radicalised. The concern was misplaced:

> What it boiled down to was that the student was becoming overly religious in their eyes, and the academic said to me things like 'the first thing I thought about over the weekend when we got the news [about the attack] was, was this student involved?'

These kinds of inappropriate referrals (even when not passed on to Prevent itself) can break down trust between staff and students and make students wary of expressing their religiosity as openly as they would like.

Conclusion

The United Kingdom's counter-terrorism approach takes an epidemiological approach, seeing extremism as a virus to which everyone is vulnerable, thus justifying the expansion of Prevent across the population (Heath-Kelly, 2017). Yet since Prevent's inception, some bodies (Muslim ones) have been seen as more vulnerable to catching the virus than others. Reliance on non-specialists to spot radicalisation has led to many inappropriate referrals, and in educational institutions risks breaking down trust between Muslims and their teachers. In response to these criticisms, in 2019 the government announced another review of Prevent; but it remains to be seen how effective this will be because its terms of reference have ruled out evaluating 'the past delivery of Prevent' (Grierson, 2019a; Home Office, 2019c).

Among universities, there is great diversity in how Prevent is implemented. Some take a minimalist, light-touch approach, complying with the law but going no further. Others adopt a much more rigorous approach. All accept the need to comply, upon which their reputation and funding depends. Yet as our research shows, some senior managers tasked with implementing Prevent remain unconvinced of its effectiveness or necessity. They recognise that radicalisation into terrorism is much rarer in universities than the popular narratives suggest, and yet they have no choice. Compliance is demanded of universities by regulators like the Office for Students.

As noted in Chapter 2, according to data submitted by universities to the OfS, in the vast majority of cases they uphold requests for events and speakers (OfS, 2019: 10). This is encouraging, but the data do not give us the full picture. The Prevent Duty Guidance encourages universities towards guarded liberalism or even no-platforming for controversial speakers, and as Spiller et al. (2018) note, some university managers have interpreted this in a 'bureaucratic conservati[ve]' way. Some may seek to discourage requests for controversial speakers informally, which would not be accounted for in their OfS data returns. Moreover, most student requests for speakers are directed not to university management but to students' unions, which must comply with charity law. As we show in Chapter 5, this additional factor is pushing some students' union staff towards risk aversion; we found clear evidence of such informal discouragement of controversial speakers.

Prevent is a major instrument imposed upon society, with poor evidence or research to suggest that extremism is common amongst Muslims. It resonates with Schmitt's insistence upon 'decisionism', by which governments decide what reality looks like, and citizens accept the government's narrative even when they themselves see no evidence for it in the norms that govern their daily lives: 'the legal order rests on a decision and not on a norm' (Schmitt, 2005: 10). Schmitt believed this was an entirely appropriate, legally justifiable and indeed necessary feature of strong government.

How problematic we find this depends on our starting assumptions about the rights and risks involved in allowing extreme or hate speech and in suppressing it. We find Strauss's 'persuasion principle' helpful: a government must not suppress speech simply because it might persuade people to accept views the government disapproves of (see Chapter 1) (Strauss, 1991). It is likely that much of the controversial though lawful speech that Prevent seeks to limit would be protected under the persuasion principle because restricting speech interferes with listeners' and speakers' autonomy. This is particularly so in the context of university events, where there is little evidence that exposure to extreme views actually leads to radicalisation.

A striking finding was that, despite working in universities, the Prevent Leads did not outline educational solutions to address the possible risk of radicalisation, even though they often raised concerns about freedom of speech: none suggested that more teaching about Islam or more structured discussions about values could help iron out confusion, discrimination or Islamophobia. Nor did they suggest that students should be included in discussion of Prevent policies. We show the need for this in Chapter 7. Additionally, most did not think that Prevent was having a negative impact on Muslims. This suggests a disconnection between Prevent Leads and Muslim students, as we see in the next chapter.

Notes

1 It is unclear if this framework also applies to Prevent Professional Concerns conferences in Scotland.
2 Further regional differences have emerged since 2018. English universities must now submit extensive annual data to the OfS about how they are complying with Prevent.

References

Legal cases

R (on the application of Salman Butt) v The Secretary of the State for the Home Department. [2019] EWCA Civ 256. https://www.judiciary.uk/wp-content/uploads/2019/03/r-butt-v-sshd-judgment.pdf.

Salman Butt v The Secretary of the State for the Home Department. [2017] EWHC 1930 (Admin). https://www.bindmans.com/uploads/files/documents/CO-6361-2015_-_Butt_v_Secretary_of_State_for_the_Home_Department_-_Final...pdf.

Secondary sources

Aked, H. (2020) *False Positives: The Prevent Counter-Extremism Policy in Healthcare.* London: Medact. https://www.medact.org/wp-content/uploads/2020/07/MEDACT-False-Positives-WEB.pdf.

BBC News (2017) 'Who Are Britain's Jihadists', 12 October. https://www.bbc.co.uk/news/uk-32026985.

Clements, J., Roberts, M. and Forman, D. (2020) *Listening to British Muslims: Policing, Extremism and Prevent.* London: Crest. https://www.crestadvisory.com/post/listening-to-british-muslims-policing-extremism-and-prevent.

Commission for Countering Extremism (2019) *Challenging Hateful Extremism.* London: Commission for Countering Extremism. https://assets.publishing.service.gov.uk/government/uploads/system/uploads/attachment_data/file/874101/200320_Challenging_Hateful_Extremism.pdf.

Commission for Countering Extremism (2020) *COVID-19: How Hateful Extremists are Exploiting the Pandemic*. https://assets.publishing.service.gov.uk/government/uploads/system/uploads/attachment_data/file/898925/CCE_Briefing_Note_001.pdf.

Communities and Local Government Committee (2010) *Preventing Violent Extremism*. House of Commons (HC 65): Sixth Report of Session 2019–10. London: The Stationery Office. https://publications.parliament.uk/pa/cm200910/cmselect/cmcomloc/65/65.pdf.

Counter-Terrorism and Security Act 2015. http://www.legislation.gov.uk/ukpga/2015/6/contents/enacted.

Dean, C. (2014) 'The Healthy Identity Intervention: The UK's Development of a Psychologically Informed Intervention to Address Extremist Offending'. In Silke, A. (ed.) *Prisons, Terrorism and Extremism*. Oxford: Routledge: 89–98.

Department for Business, Innovation and Skills, Home Office, Prime Minister's Office, The Right Hon David Cameron and The Right Hon Jo Johnson (2015) 'PM's Extremism Taskforce: Tackling Extremism in Universities and Colleges Top of the Agenda'. Press release, 17 September. https://www.gov.uk/government/news/pms-extremism-taskforce-tackling-extremism-in-universities-and-colleges-top-of-the-agenda.

Department for Education (2014) 'Guidance on Promoting British Values in Schools Published'. Press release, 27 November. https://www.gov.uk/government/news/guidance-on-promoting-british-values-in-schools-published.

Greenwood, G., Stein, J. and Hamilton, F. (2020) 'Children under 6 Referred to Extremism Programme', *The Times*, 2 May. https://www.thetimes.co.uk/article/children-under-6-referred-to-extremism-programme-c3vlzf56s.

Greer, S. and Bell, L. (2018) 'Counter-Terrorist Law in British Universities: A Review of the "Prevent" Debate', *Public Law*, January: 84–105. http://www.bristol.ac.uk/media-library/sites/law/GreerBell%20PREVENT%20final%20article.pdf.

Grierson, J. (2019a) 'Prevent Review Branded "Superficial" as Past Decisions Overlooked', *The Guardian*, 16 September. https://www.theguardian.com/uk-news/2019/sep/16/prevent-review-branded-superficial-as-past-decisions-overlooked.

Grierson, J. (2019b) 'Counter-Terror Police Running Secret Prevent Database', *The Guardian*, 6 October. https://www.theguardian.com/uk-news/2019/oct/06/counter-terror-police-are-running-secret-prevent-database.

Grove, J. (2015) 'No 10's Extremism Report Mirrors Text of Thinktank Study', *Times Higher Education*, 1 October. https://www.timeshighereducation.com/news/no-10s-extremism-report-mirrors-text-thinktank-study.

Guest, M., Aune, K., Sharma S. and Warner, R. (2013) *Christianity and the University Experience: Understanding Student Faith*. London: Bloomsbury.

Hardy, K. (2018) 'Comparing Theories of Radicalisation with Countering Violent Extremism Policy', *Journal for Deradicalization*, 15, Summer: 76–110. https://journals.sfu.ca/jd/index.php/jd/article/view/150.

Heath-Kelly, C. (2017) 'The Geography of Pre-Criminal Space: Epidemiological Imaginations of Radicalisation Risk in the UK Prevent Strategy, 2007–2017', *Critical Studies on Terrorism*, 10, 2: 297–319. https://www.tandfonline.com/doi/full/10.1080/17539153.2017.1327141.

Holmwood, J. and O'Toole, T. (2017) *Countering Extremism in British Schools? The Truth about the Birmingham Trojan Horse Affair*. Bristol: Policy Press.

Home Office (2006) *Countering International Terrorism: The United Kingdom's Strategy*. London: The Stationery Office. https://assets.publishing.service.gov.uk/government/uploads/system/uploads/attachment_data/file/272320/6888.pdf.

Home Office (2009) *The United Kingdom's Strategy for Countering International Terrorism*. London: The Stationery Office. https://assets.publishing.service.gov.uk/government/uploads/system/uploads/attachment_data/file/228644/7547.pdf.

Home Office (2011a) *CONTEST: The United Kingdom's Strategy for Countering Terrorism*. London: HM Government. https://assets.publishing.service.gov.uk/government/uploads/system/uploads/attachment_data/file/97994/contest-summary.pdf.

Home Office (2011b) *Prevent Strategy*. House of Commons Cm 8092. London: The Stationery Office. https://ww.gov.uk/government/publications/prevent-strategy-2011.

Home Office (2012) *Channel: Vulnerability Assessment Network*. https://assets.publishing.service.gov.uk/government/uploads/system/uploads/attachment_data/file/118187/vul-assessment.pdf.

Home Office (2015a) *Prevent Duty Guidance*. London: The Stationery Office. https://www.gov.uk/government/publications/prevent-duty-guidance/prevent-duty-guidance-for-higher-education-institutions-in-england-and-wales.

Home Office (2015b) *Channel Duty Guidance: Protecting Vulnerable People from Being Drawn into Terrorism*. London: The Stationery Office. https://assets.publishing.service.gov.uk/government/uploads/system/uploads/attachment_data/file/425189/Channel_Duty_Guidance_April_2015.pdf.

Home Office (2018) *CONTEST: The United Kingdom's Strategy for Countering Terrorism*. House of Commons Cm 9608. London: HM Government. https://assets.publishing.service.gov.uk/government/uploads/system/uploads/attachment_data/file/716907/140618_CCS207_CCS0218929798-1_CONTEST_3.0_WEB.pdf.

Home Office (2019a) *Prevent Duty Guidance: For Higher Education Institutions in England and Wales*. Updated 10 April. https://www.gov.uk/government/publications/prevent-duty-guidance/prevent-duty-guidance-for-higher-education-institutions-in-england-and-wales.

Home Office (2019b) 'Individuals Referred to and Supported through the Prevent Programme, England and Wales, April 2018 to March 2019', *Home Office Statistical Bulletin*, 32, 19. https://assets.publishing.service.gov.uk/government/uploads/system/uploads/attachment_data/file/853646/individuals-referred-supported-prevent-programme-apr2018-mar2019-hosb3219.pdf.

Home Office (2019c) *Independent Review of Prevent*. London: Home Office. https://www.gov.uk/government/collections/independent-review-of-prevent.

Home Office (n.d.-a) 'Consent from Individual'. https://www.elearning.prevent.homeoffice.gov.uk/channel_awareness/12-consent-from-the-individual.html.

Home Office (n.d.-b) 'Completing the Picture'. https://www.elearning.prevent.homeoffice.gov.uk/prevent_referrals/11-completing-the-picture.html.

Home Office (n.d.-c) 'Prevent Safeguarding Referral Form'. https://www.elearning.prevent.homeoffice.gov.uk/prevent_referrals/resources/Prevent-Example-Referral-Form-CAMPUS.pdf.

House of Commons Home Affairs Committee (2012) *Roots of Violent Radicalisation*. Nineteenth Report of Session 2010–12, vol. 1. London: The Stationery Office. https://publications.parliament.uk/pa/cm201012/cmselect/cmhaff/1446/1446.pdf.

Joint Committee on Human Rights (2016) *Counter-Extremism*. House of Lords/House of Commons (HL Paper 39; HC 105): Second Report of Session 2016–17. London: The Stationery Office. https://publications.parliament.uk/pa/jt201617/jtselect/jtrights/105/105.pdf.

Joint Committee on Human Rights (JCHR) (2017) *Freedom of Speech in Universities*. House of Lords/House of Commons (HC 589). Oral evidence, 6 December. London: The Stationery Office. http://data.parliament.uk/writtenevidence/committeeevidence.svc/evidencedocument/human-rights-committee/freedom-of-speech-in-universities/oral/75335.pdf.

Joint Committee on Human Rights (JCHR) (2018) *Freedom of Speech in Universities*. House of Lords/House of Commons (HC 589; HL Paper 111): Fourth Report of Session 2017–19. London: The Stationery Office. https://publications.parliament.uk/pa/jt201719/jtselect/jtrights/589/589.pdf.

Lloyd, M. (2016) 'Structured Guidelines for Assessing Risk in Extremist Offenders', *Assessment & Development Matters*, 8, 2: 15–18.

Lloyd, M. and Dean, C. (2015) 'The Development of Structured Guidelines for Assessing Risk in Extremist Offenders', *Journal of Threat Assessment and Management*, 2, 1: 40–52.

Morey, P. and Alibhai-Brown, Y. (2016) *Trust and the Prevent Duty*. PaCCS Policy Briefing. Partnership for Conflict, Crime and Security Research. http://www.paccsresearch.org.uk/policy-briefings/trust-and-the-prevent-duty/files/assets/common/downloads/PaCCS%20Trust%20and%20the%20Prevent%20Duty.pdf.

Muslim Council of Britain (2019) 'Muslim Council of Britain Responds to Prevent Review Legal Challenge'. Press release, 20 December. https://mcb.org.uk/press-releases/mcb-responds-to-prevent-review-legal-challenge/.

National Offender Management Service. (2011) *Extremism Risk Guidance. ERG22+ Structured Professional Guidelines for Assessing Risk of Extremist Offending*. London: Ministry of Justice.

O'Donnell, A (2016) 'Securitisation, Counterterrorism and the Silencing of Dissent: The Educational Implications of *Prevent*', *British Journal of Educational Studies*, 64, 1: 53–76. https://www.tandfonline.com/doi/abs/10.1080/00071005.2015.1121201.

O'Toole, T., Meer, N., de Hanas, D.N., Jones, S.H. and Modood, T. (2016) 'Governing through Prevent? Regulation and Contested Practice in State–Muslim Engagement', *Sociology*, 50, 1: 160–177. https://journals.sagepub.com/doi/10.1177/0038038514564437.

Office for Students (OfS) (2019) *Prevent Monitoring Accountability and Data Returns 2017–18: Evaluation Report*. London: Office for Students. https://www.officeforstudents.org.uk/media/860e26e2-63e7-47eb-84e0-49100788009c/ofs2019_22.pdf.

Powis, B., Randhawa-Horne, K. and Bishopp, D. (2019) *An Examination of the Structural Properties of the Extremism Risk Guidelines (ERG22+): A Structured Formulation Tool for Extremist Offenders, Terrorism and Political Violence*. London: Ministry of Justice. https://assets.publishing.service.gov.uk/government/uploads/system/uploads/attachment_data/file/816507/the-structural-properties-of-the-extremism-risk-guidelines-ERG22.pdf.

Qurashi, F. (2017) '"Just Get on with It": Implementing the Prevent Duty in Higher Education and the Role of Academic Expertise', *Education, Citizenship, and Social Justice*, 12, 3: 197–212. https://journals.sagepub.com/doi/abs/10.1177/1746197917716106.

Qureshi, A. (2016) *The Science of Pre-Crime: The Secret 'Radicalisation' Study Underpinning Prevent*. London: CAGE. https://www.cage.ngo/product/the-science-of-pre-crime-report.

Rashid, N. (2016) *Veiled Threats: Representing the Muslim Woman in Public Policy Discourses*. Bristol: Policy Press.

Ross, A. (2016) 'Academics Criticise Anti-radicalisation Strategy in Open Letter', *The Guardian*, 29 September. https://www.theguardian.com/uk-news/2016/sep/29/academics-criticise-prevent-anti-radicalisation-strategy-open-letter.

Royal College of Psychiatrists (2016) *Counter-terrorism and Psychiatry*. Position Statement PS04/16. https://www.rcpsych.ac.uk/docs/default-source/improving-care/better-mh-policy/position-statements/ps04_16.pdf?sfvrsn=a6681467_2.

Scarcella, A., Page, R. and Furtado, V. (2016) 'Terrorism, Radicalisation, Extremism, Authoritarianism and Fundamentalism: A Systematic Review of the Quality and Psychometric Properties of Assessments', *PLOS ONE*, 11, 12. https://journals.plos.org/plosone/article?id=10.1371/journal.pone.0166947.

Schmitt, C. (2005) *Political Theology*. Translated by G. Schwab. London: University of Chicago Press.

Scott-Baumann, A., Bloomfield. A. and Roughton. L. (2000) *Becoming a Secondary School Teacher*. London: Hodder and Stoughton.

Scott-Baumann, A. and Tomlinson, H. (2016) 'Cultural Cold Wars: The Risk of Anti-"extremism" Policy for Academic Freedom of Expression'. *SOAS*, 15 June. https://blogs.soas.ac.uk/muslimwise/2016/06/15/question-time-cultural-cold-wars-the-risk-of-anti-extremism-policy-for-academic-freedom-of-expression-alison-scott-baumann-and-hugh-tomlinson-qc/.

Skinner, B.F. (1988) *About Behaviourism*. New York: Random House.

Slater, A. (2018) 'Challenging the Legitimacy of Extremism'. In Panjwani, F., Revell, L., Gholami, R. and Diboll, M. (eds.) *Education and Extremisms: Rethinking Liberal Pedagogies in the Contemporary World*. Abingdon: Routledge: 91–104.

Spiller, K., Awan, I. and Whiting, A. (2018) 'What Does Terrorism Look Like?' University Lecturers' Interpretations of Their Prevent Duties and Tackling Extremism in UK Universities', *Critical Studies on Terrorism*, 11, 1: 130–150. https://www.tandfonline.com/doi/abs/10.1080/17539153.2017.1396954.

Strauss, D.A. (1991) 'Persuasion, Autonomy, and Freedom of Expression', *Columbia Law Review*, 91: 334–371. https://core.ac.uk/download/pdf/207571931.pdf.

Stuart, H. (2017) *Islamist Terrorism: Analysis of Offences and Attacks in the UK (1998–2015)*. London: The Henry Jackson Society. http://henryjacksonsociety.org/wp-content/uploads/2017/03/Islamist-Terrorism-preview-1.pdf.

Sutton, R. (2015) *Preventing Prevent? Challenges to Counter-Radicalisation Policy on Campus*. London: The Henry Jackson Society. http://henryjacksonsociety.org/wp-content/uploads/2015/10/Preventing-Prevent_webversion3.pdf.

Swann, S., De Simone, D. and Sandford, D. (2019) 'At Least Seven from my University Joined IS, Says Captured Fighter', *BBC News*, 1 April. https://www.bbc.co.uk/news/uk-47772772.

Thomas, P. (2014) 'Divorced but Still Co-habiting? Britain's Prevent/Community Cohesion Policy Tension', *British Politics*, 9, 4: 472–493. https://link.springer.com/article/10.1057/bp.2014.16.

Townsend, M. (2017) 'Theresa May's Counter-terrorism Bill Close to "Sinking without Trace"', *The Guardian*, 29 January. https://www.theguardian.com/politics/2017/jan/29/theresa-may-counter-terrorism-bill-sinking-without-trace-extremism-british-values.

Universities UK (2018) *Written Evidence from Universities UK*. In Joint Committee on Human Rights (2018) *Freedom of Speech in Universities*. Written evidence, FSU0010. http://data.parliament.uk/WrittenEvidence/CommitteeEvidence.svc/EvidenceDocument/Human%20Rights%20Joint%20Committee/Freedom%20of%20Speech%20in%20Universities/written/75384.html.

Waldron, J. (2012) *The Harm in Hate Speech*. Cambridge, MA: Harvard University Press.

4 External agitators and students' views about freedom of speech and Prevent

The binary narrative of moral panic about universities – that, on the one hand, they are shutting down freedom of speech, and that on the other, they are allowing too much freedom for extremists – is driven by powerful voices outside Higher Education. In this chapter we expose the factually weak yet emotive analyses used by two particularly influential organisations: the Henry Jackson Society, a neoconservative foreign policy think tank founded in 2005, and *Spiked*, an online libertarian magazine with some right-wing bias, founded in 2001. These organisations influence public discourse to push students away from the liberal approach to freedom of speech and towards the extremes of no-platforming and libertarianism, respectively.

We contrast these external organisations' flawed analyses with robust research evidence into students' own views about free speech on campus – including their views about the Prevent Duty. We draw in particular on findings from a major research project funded by the Arts and Humanities Research Council (AHRC) and led by Alison Scott-Baumann: *Re/presenting Islam on Campus* (2015–18).

The Henry Jackson Society: no-platforming extremism

Some external organisations push students towards the no-platforming approach to freedom of speech, in the name of counter-terrorism. These depict students as reckless, naïvely inviting extreme speakers who pose a significant risk of radicalising them. Particularly important in this regard is the Henry Jackson Society (HJS). Its activities in Higher Education include its media work in defence of Prevent and its Student Rights project, which analyses the supposed presence of extremism on campuses.

Its work has significantly influenced recent governments. For example, in order to highlight radicalisation in universities, the 2011 iteration of the Prevent Strategy quoted statistics from a HJS report about the backgrounds of people convicted of Islamist-related terror offences between 1999 and 2010. Most were guilty of offences such as facilitating, inciting or showing an interest in terrorism, rather than actually committing or preparing to commit an attack. Moreover, the report showed that only 13 (9%) of convicted offenders had been in Further or Higher Education at the time of their offence or charge (Home Office, 2011: 72; Simcox et al., 2011: xi–xii). As we saw in Chapter 3, another HJS report was closely paraphrased in the 2015 press release from Downing Street introducing the Prevent Duty, showing a clear link between HJS material and the government's Extremism Analysis Unit (Department for Business, Innovation and Skills et al., 2015).

HJS has faced repeated accusations of bias against Islam, and (according to analysis by Spinwatch, an organisation that investigates Public Relations and lobbying) of being part of a transatlantic 'Islamophobia network' (Bridge Initiative Team, 2018). A number of senior HJS staff (including its former associate director, Douglas Murray, and the founder of Student Rights, Raheem Kassam) have expressed hostile views towards immigration, Islam as a religion, and sometimes Muslims as people. Murray (2017) warned that Muslim immigration was causing *The Strange Death of Europe*, while Kassam (2017) argued that Western Muslims are creating 'No Go Zones' where 'sharia law' dominates; his book was endorsed by Nigel Farage, for whom Kassam has worked as a senior adviser (Payne, 2015). These books appeal to right-wing populist, alarmist narratives about Muslims and position themselves as defenders of freedom of speech, implying that they express what others dare not say.

While most of HJS's work on extremism has focused on Islamist extremism, it has expanded recently to cover far-right extremism as well (Ehsan and Stott, 2020a, 2020b). Ironically, the right-wing news outlet *Breitbart News* claimed this has damaged HJS's reputation for being a critical voice against Islam (Bokhari, 2020).

To explore the role of HJS in the debate about extremism and freedom of speech on campus, we look in detail at a report it published in 2019: *Extreme Speakers and Events: In the 2017/18 Academic Year*. It claimed that extremists have 'near-unfettered' access to students on campus, and that there has been 'an industrial-scale failure by universities to apply their Prevent duties' (Fox, 2019a, 2019b). Upon hearing this, the Conservative MP Robert Halfon called for an 'urgent inquiry' (Gilligan, 2019). Yet HJS's claims about a lack of compliance with the Prevent Duty run counter to the assessment by the Office for Students

(OfS) that in 2017–18, all but two English universities met their statutory Prevent Duty (OfS, 2019). Moreover, as Perfect and Scott-Baumann (2019) demonstrate, the *Extreme Speakers* report has serious methodological flaws which make its conclusions highly suspect.

For instance, the report's data come from HJS's monitoring of university events advertised online, rather than from attendance at them. Consequently, it provides no evidence that speakers at these events actually made extreme remarks. The report collects data selectively, focusing almost entirely on speakers invited by Muslim students' societies (93% of the 204 reported events focused on Islam or Muslims). Other religious societies, such as some Christian Unions, also host speakers with socially conservative views (Guest et al., 2013; Perfect et al., 2019: 108–109), but HJS does not assess such speakers with the same criteria as for Muslims.

Extreme Speakers repeatedly presents socially conservative remarks as evidence of extremism. Some speakers are reported to disagree with same-sex relations or to have made homophobic comments in the past, which many people would find deeply abhorrent. However, undoubtedly a small but significant minority of the population (of all religions and beliefs) share such views, which are not necessarily unlawful. It is questionable whether the term 'extremism' should apply to all these people. Moreover, there is no reason why universities should assess such a speaker as posing a risk of leading others into terrorism (the focus of Prevent).

In some cases, the HJS report presents speakers' past remarks misleadingly, in ways that obscure crucial context. For example, it states that a university speaker, Muhammad Taqi Usmani, had previously claimed that 'Islam allowed the taking of slaves with the condition that it is in a jihad sanctioned by the Shari'ah against the disbelievers' (Fox, 2019b: 93). The lack of context means the impression is given that Usmani advocates slavery. In fact, the statement was written many years before the 2018 university event, in an encyclopaedic commentary (originally in Arabic) analysing the Hadith collection of 9th-century scholar Sahih Muslim. Usmani argues that though classical Islamic scripture permits slavery, historically Islam transformed slavery into an institution 'of mutual love and brotherhood' and encouraged the freeing of slaves because 'freedom is more desirable in the Islamic Shari'ah' than slavery (Usmani, 2013). This hardly amounts to an endorsement of slavery today.

On closer inspection, this speaker has conservative interpretations of religious scripture, which are open to debate. But why offering such interpretations amounts to 'opposition to fundamental British values' (the government's definition of extremism) is unclear. Universities asked to host such speakers might reasonably decide to adopt a guarded liberal approach when facilitating the events, but preventing them from speaking entirely (as HJS encourages) removes the option of open debate. Altogether, the report exemplifies the flawed strategies now common in public debate: taking opponents' past remarks out of context; applying the sticky label of 'extremism' to them based on comments made years previously; or labelling them extreme by association with others rather than based on their own remarks. For these reasons it does not reliably indicate the extent of extremism in universities; it is therefore worrying that the government and journalists have uncritically accepted HJS's analysis.

HJS's implication is that universities should refuse to host speakers with these controversial views by default – a position similar to Sorial (2012) and Waldron (2012). In fact, this goes further towards the no-platforming approach of freedom of speech than the Prevent Duty itself since, as shown in Chapter 3, the courts have clarified that the Duty does not prohibit universities from hosting extreme speakers. HJS assumes that students must be shielded from controversial ideas, as they are incapable of critiquing them. Encouraging such risk aversion undermines the core purpose of universities.

Spiked: libertarian traffic lights

In contrast to HJS, *Spiked*, the online political magazine, pushes students in the opposite direction, towards the anti-interventionist, libertarian approach to freedom of speech, with few restrictions on either the content of what can be discussed or on the language that can be used. *Spiked* argues that universities and students are unfairly shutting down free speech – especially for politically conservative and libertarian voices. Between 2015 and 2018, *Spiked* published an annual traffic light ranking of British universities in terms of their level of speech, using an index to categorise them as either 'green' (not restrictive of freedom of speech within the law), 'red' (actively censorious), or 'amber' (freedom of speech is chilled through excessive regulation). In 2018, for example, it gave a red rating to over half of its sample of 115 universities and a green rating to only 6% (Spiked Online, 2018: 1–2). It has also sought to generate grassroots support for libertarianism on campus, by encouraging students to establish free speech societies to push back against regulations on campus (Slater, 2019).

This forms part of *Spiked*'s campaign against restrictions on freedom of speech in society more widely and against institutions it perceives as failing to uphold liberalism. *Spiked* is characterised by its anti-interventionist stance, which resonates with strong beliefs about personal autonomy and the right to be offensive. These beliefs resemble the neoliberal 'marketplace of ideas' thinking that advocates a free-for-all of self-expression. Their approach also adopts the right-wing populist attack upon rights: minority rights are over-protected, so majority rights must fight back.

Spiked's university rankings have been extremely influential among politicians and media commentators and are often cited as fact without further interrogation (Bennett, 2017). This fuels the popular narrative of moral panic that students are illiberal 'snowflakes' who overprotect minority rights and cannot tolerate opposing views. However, the methodology underpinning the rankings undermines their credibility (Thompson, 2018). *Spiked* relies on examination of university and students' union policies, searching for perceived excessive caution, and on media reportage of censorious student action (where available), rather than on any analysis of whether these policies or actions actually impede freedom of speech on the ground. In some cases *Spiked* marks universities down for policies or actions that have little significance for debate on campus.

For example, in 2018 Royal Holloway, University of London was given a 'red' ranking by *Spiked* because of policies that prohibit 'jokes, gossip, letters or other comments ... which could reasonably be regarded as offensive'; that prohibit 'transphobic propaganda'; and that warn against over-indulgence in alcohol. It is unknown how these policies were interpreted by staff in practice. For example, it is unclear whether the university understood 'transphobic propaganda' as meaning material likely to be unlawful under anti-discrimination law (in which case, the university's policy was simply compliance with the law), or whether staff would also censure lawful material that might nonetheless be offensive to trans people (Slater, 2019). While *Spiked* has highlighted policies that indicate a tendency to guarded liberalism among some universities, its lack of data about how these policies were interpreted, and how they actually affected students, means the rankings have no reliability for measuring the state of free speech in universities.

The implication from *Spiked*'s ranking is that universities and students' unions are out of step with the general public, and with other sectors like workplaces, in terms of freedom of speech. But many of the policies *Spiked* flags as problematic are widely accepted. Prohibitions on 'unwanted sexual comments' are commonplace in the workplace – indeed such comments sometimes amount to crimes – but Royal Holloway's students' union is marked down for giving 'zero tolerance' to such statements. Part of *Spiked*'s approach has been to present its own very libertarian, anti-interventionist stance on speech as normative, but in fact public attitudes are split. According to a poll conducted for the think tank Theos in 2019, 44% of British adults think universities should always support freedom of speech within the law, even for extreme speakers, and 35% think there are some views that are so offensive that universities should not allow them (Perfect et al., 2019: 10).

Overall, *Spiked*'s ranking system has overplayed the scale of the problem in universities, which has helped drive moral panic about the sector. There is not a full crisis of freedom of speech on campus. However, as we show in the following sections, there is important research evidence confirming that *some* students and staff do feel their freedom of speech is constrained.

Students' views about freedom of speech in university

With organisations like HJS and *Spiked* shaping public perception of students, students' own views about freedom of speech are often ignored. Two nationally representative surveys of students reveal what is actually going on.

The first, commissioned by the Higher Education Policy Institute (HEPI) in 2016, found that 83% of 1,006 undergraduates felt free to express their views on campus, while 12% did not. Moreover, 60% stated that universities should never limit freedom of speech. However, they were more likely to support a libertarian or liberal approach to free speech when asked about it as an abstract principle; when asked about specific campus policies that might affect it, 43% thought that protecting minorities from discrimination can be more important than unlimited freedom of expression. Strikingly, 27% of respondents thought that the UK Independence Party (UKIP) should be banned from speaking at universities (Hillman, 2016: 7, 11, 17, 41). No doubt many were worried about alleged racism within UKIP (later in 2016, UKIP leader Nigel Farage unveiled his infamous 'Breaking Point' anti-migrant poster) (Stewart and Mason, 2016). Nonetheless, it is concerning that over a quarter of students would ban a major right-wing party. This shows the necessity of explicit teaching on campus about the range of options for handling freedom of speech, beyond the simple binary of libertarian and no-platforming approaches.

The second survey was commissioned by the Policy Institute of King's College London (KCL) in 2019. An overwhelming majority of its 2,153 respondents thought it was important for universities to protect freedom of speech, and 70% felt comfortable expressing their views at university. Strikingly, they were much more likely to think that freedom of speech is threatened in the United Kingdom overall (54%) than in their university (23%) (Grant et al., 2019: 8; 14). However, as in the HEPI survey, a minority (25%) said they felt unable to express their views at university because they were 'scared of disagreeing with my peers'. Right-leaning or Brexit-supporting students (including 34% of Conservative Party supporters and 32% of Leave supporters) were more likely to feel this way than left-leaning or Remain-supporting students. About 20% of the latter two groups also felt unable to express their views, which shows it is not only those on the right who feel their freedom to speak is chilled – contrary to the impression given by right-wing populist leaders (Grant et al., 2019: 7–16). Other research suggests that many Jewish students feel uncomfortable engaging in debate about the Israel/Palestine conflict on campus, for example, out of fear of being criticised for failing to condemn the Israeli government's policies (National Union of Students, 2018; Perfect et al., 2019: 140–141).

Respondents to the KCL survey, as with the HEPI one, tended to combine liberal views concerning the principle of freedom of speech with support for policies that may limit it (guarded liberal or no-platforming views). Most, for example, thought that universities have the right to ban people 'with extreme views' from speaking, should be able to restrict the expression of 'political views that are upsetting or offensive to certain groups', and should balance each 'controversial speaker' with another with an 'opposing view'. A majority also thought it important to be part of a university community where 'I am not exposed to intolerant and offensive ideas' – a sentiment implying strong guarded liberalism (Grant et al., 2019: 17).

The KCL report is particularly helpful for two reasons. First, it reveals the diversity of student views about free speech. It distinguishes between three categories of students: the 'Activist' (23% of the sample), the 'Libertarian' (20%) and the 'Contented' (56%). It defines Activists as those who feel strongly about protecting students from harmful views, Libertarians as those who think safe space culture poses a threat to freedom of speech, and the Contented as those who do not have particularly strong views either way. Activist and Contented students feel strongly that freedom of speech is protected in their university, but over half of Libertarians feel it is threatened. Most Activist (73%) and Contented (65%) students think they should be shielded from offensive views, compared to only 40% of Libertarians (Grant et al., 2019: 3; 31–33). This is still a sizeable proportion of students categorised as Libertarian-leaning who support guarded liberalism – suggesting that these are not full-blooded libertarians, despite their desire for greater freedom of speech. It appears students can consistently and simultaneously affirm seemingly contradictory positions about this issue.

Second, the researchers compared their student survey with a survey of the general public conducted at the same time. Contrary to the assumptions of *Spiked*, students and the wider public had similar views on the overall value of freedom of speech, with an overwhelming majority of each group expressing its importance. A sizeable minority of students (35%) felt that 'safe spaces' and a culture of 'safetyism' threaten freedom of speech in universities, compared to 44% of the general public (Grant et al., 2019: 3; 21). This shows that public concerns about safe space culture are shared on campus – but also that people outside the university sector, with less recent experience of it, are more worried about this than students themselves; we believe this is a result of misleading media portrayals of campus life, as most members of the public have no direct experience of student activities.

Finally, 26% of students thought it is acceptable to use 'physical violence' to prevent people from expressing hate speech – but students are not unique in this because 20% of the public agreed (Grant et al., 2019: 22). These alarming figures show how essential it is to provide better education about handling offensive views calmly, both within the university sector and outside it.

The AHRC *Re/presenting Islam on Campus* project – students' views about freedom of speech, Islam and Islamophobia

In the next two sections we fill in the gap in information on what Muslim students think about freedom of speech, particularly in relation to Prevent. We draw on findings from the *Re/presenting Islam on Campus* project (2015–18), which explored how Islam is represented and understood on UK university campuses, and the experiences of Muslims. It involved qualitative research undertaken in 2016–17 at four universities and two Muslim colleges (one broadly Shi'a and one Sunni, both with courses validated by mainstream universities). At these six sites, a total of 253 staff and students (about half of whom were Muslim) were interviewed or participated in focus groups, amounting to 140 hours of audio material. The project included a nationally representative survey of 2,022 undergraduates and postgraduates attending 132 UK universities, conducted in 2017 (Guest et al., 2020: 11). This is the largest multi-method study of Islam on campus to date, building on other research on Muslim students' experiences (e.g., Brown and Saeed, 2015).

The AHRC project found similar attitudes to freedom of speech among students as reported by HEPI and KCL. Only 12% of survey respondents, including 9% of Muslim respondents, thought that universities should have the ability to limit freedom of expression within the law. This challenges the popular narrative that Muslims value freedom of speech less than non-Muslims. At the same time, most respondents insisted that protecting minorities from discrimination and ensuring their dignity can be more important than unlimited free speech (Guest et al., 2020: 56). This combined a liberal view of the principle of freedom of speech with a guarded liberal approach to handling it practically. Strikingly, Muslim students were more likely than non-Muslims to view guarded liberal anti-discrimination measures as more important than unlimited freedom of speech. When combined with the findings from the interviews and focus groups, it was clear that many felt that libertarianism would lead to expressions that offend or victimise them or other minorities (Guest et al., 2020: 56).

The research also considered students' impressions of Muslims and Islam. UK students have a positive view of Muslims as people, with most survey respondents agreeing that 'Muslims have made a valuable contribution to British life'. Yet about a fifth believe that 'Islam is incompatible with British values', and 43% – including 17% of Muslim students – believe that Islam is a religion that discriminates against women (Guest et al., 2020: 28). Students are more likely than the general population to view Islam positively, but a significant proportion retain concerns about it. Such issues need to be discussed, not avoided. Universities need to do more to challenge misconceptions or prejudice against Muslims, whilst making space for frank debate about religions and beliefs.

The *Re/presenting Islam on Campus* research also showed that universities should do more to ensure Muslims are not treated unfairly on campus. While many Muslim students feel safe in universities, a minority feel vulnerable to abuse. The qualitative research found evidence of prejudice against Muslims – including among some university staff – as well as of verbal and physical discrimination and racism. Muslim and non-Muslim interviewees alike often discussed clothing and physical appearance – in particular, hijabs and beards – and Muslims understood these as markers that could lead to them being viewed by others with suspicion (Guest et al., 2020: 29). These findings corroborate the results of a 2018 National Union of Students (NUS) survey of Muslim students. A third of the 578 respondents were worried about experiencing abuse on campus – particularly Muslim women who wore religious coverings – and a quarter said they had experienced abuse or a crime on campus, which they believed was motivated by prejudice against their Muslim identity. In addition, half of the survey respondents had faced abuse online (NUS, 2018: 18–19; Perfect et al., 2019: 137–138). Saeed clarifies the powerful effect of Islamophobia on Muslim students who experience it; not only are they discriminated against but they internalise the understanding of being treated as different, even dangerous. Universities are well placed to disrupt such loss of agency and replace it with strong arguments about citizenship and belonging (Saeed, 2019: 175–187).

Discrimination on campus takes gendered forms (Phoenix, 2020), with Muslim women more likely than men to experience Islamophobia. It is necessary to reverse the asymmetrical cognitive burden experienced by Muslim women, who are often forced to bear their gendered identity as an impediment on university campuses, where they may be perceived as less intellectually capable than their peers (Guest et al., 2020). Women's transformative interventions into academic discourses on Islam are also hindered because the study of Islam is dominated by men in UK universities and Islamic colleges (Naguib, 2020).

Luke (1994) notes that sometimes women remain silent in public discussion as a strategic 'refusal of patriarchy' and thus a way to 'subvert and resist' (Luke, 1994: 222, 214). In the university context, however, this is counterproductive and deprives women of vital educational interaction. Like us, Luke recommends communal attempts at learning, instead of what she calls 'silent postcards from the edge' (1994: 227). Universities need to do more to ensure that female students from minority backgrounds feel able to speak freely in classroom and other debate settings, and part of this requires explicit discussion on campus about the extent to which women's voices are under-represented or silenced. Telis et al. (2019) found that public discussion of relative female under-participation in Q&A sessions, regardless of the reasons for it, can improve rates of questioning by women in academic settings. Such insights are important for developing a Community of Inquiry (CofI).

Finally, the *Re/presenting Islam on Campus* project revealed that there is little teaching about Islam across much of the university sector. Of the university modules on Islam and Muslims, 66% are taught at just 20 universities. A number of student and staff participants called for more university curriculum coverage and interfaith programmes that could provide a strong antidote to negative media and patriarchal discourses about Islam (Nielsen, 2000; Naguib, 2020).

Universities should work, as the feminist scholar Saba Mahmood argues (2005), to improve understandings of Islam.

Students' views about the Prevent Duty

Over half the 253 students and staff (both Muslim and non-Muslim) who participated in the AHRC-funded *Re/presenting Islam on Campus* project commented negatively about the Prevent Duty, or described it spontaneously as having a chilling effect on freedom of speech (Scott-Baumann et al., 2020). Many Muslim participants saw it as targeting them and as something that sought to monitor their behaviour. As a student who identified as both Jewish and Muslim explained:

> [M]any people know about the Prevent policy, which is the government anti-radicalisation policy, which has turned a lot of mosques and prayer rooms in universities into kind of, like, quite surveilled spaces.

A Shi'a student felt similarly, fearing that Prevent encouraged people to make false connections between religion and extremism:

> The government has singled out on the Islamic element ... So you hear sort of talk that a person who practises, merrily practises all his obligatories, acts of worship, is looked at as an extremist.

Such sentiments were expressed repeatedly in the qualitative research. As a result of Prevent, some Muslim students and staff fear being stigmatised, labelled extremist or subjected to discrimination.

The AHRC project found that Prevent does indeed have a chilling effect on freedom of speech on campus. Indeed, some people cited their worries about Prevent and their fear of drawing attention to themselves as a reason not to be part of the research. Many of those who chose to take part (both Muslim and non-Muslim) were concerned that Prevent is leading some Muslims to self-censor in the classroom, out of concern they may be deemed extremist (Guest et al., 2020: 55–56). Some Muslim participants expressed their own risk aversion in the interviews; as an Iranian male Shi'a student said:

> I know my religion is totally the opposite to what they think, so it doesn't affect my work, but the only thing it may affect is ... say if I'm putting something forward in a group, I think twice, if I should put this in this group or if I just leave it.

Others reported a pressure to self-censor among their Muslim peers:

> [T] he only practical day to day thing that affected us a lot about Prevent was the impact that it had on Muslim students. So, mentally, a lot of Muslim students became quite scared, they didn't really know what was going on, they felt like they were being targeted. It felt like they couldn't say as much as they used to because, 'Oh, what if it got reported, what if…'.
> (Female Sunni Arab Students' Union Officer)

Some students and staff also reported feeling they needed to avoid exploring controversial topics related to Islam or terrorism in their work, fearing that doing so would arouse unfair suspicion (Guest et al., 2020: 42).

These findings tally with other studies about Muslim students. A third of respondents to the 2018 NUS survey of Muslim students said they had been negatively affected by Prevent, with 14% saying their experience of Prevent had made it harder for them to express their opinions (NUS, 2018: 12). Perfect et al. (2019) found similar concerns in their research into faith and belief-related student societies. In this study for the think tank Theos, some members of Islamic Societies said they needed to be risk-averse, such as by not requesting speakers who may be perceived as controversial. Some interviewees had heard rumours about the closure of prayer rooms at other universities and feared it could happen to them if they inspired controversy. The rumours turned out to be inaccurate, but fed into a cross-university narrative that pushed Muslims into risk aversion – including students who said they had not *directly* experienced unfair scrutiny as a result of Prevent (Perfect et al., 2019: 81, 116–118).

In the AHRC-funded *Re/presenting Islam on Campus* survey of 2,022 students attending 132 universities, a striking 59% of all respondents had 'never heard of Prevent'. Muslim respondents were more likely than non-Muslims to have heard of it, but over half said they had not (Guest et al., 2020: 43). Interestingly, of respondents (Muslim and non-Muslim) with no prior awareness of Prevent, two-fifths still offered an opinion about it (based on a description given in the survey). Of the 59% who had never heard of Prevent, 16% considered it essential in universities, showing the influence of the popular narrative that radicalisation is a problem in universities, even among students with little knowledge about counter-terrorism. Moreover, there is a clear association between approval of Prevent and disapproval of Islam: of those students who view Prevent as essential in universities,

36% believe that Islam preaches intolerance towards non-Muslims, and 58% believe Islam discriminates against women. The figures for those who believe Prevent is damaging to universities, on the other hand, are 13% and 32%, respectively. This suggests the government's counter-terrorism strategy can reinforce existing negative stereotypes about Muslims among students as well as discouraging discussion that could resolve such negativity (Guest et al., 2020: 47, 52–53).

The evidence shows that students generally have low awareness about Prevent. Nonetheless, a significant minority have concerns about it. Some (though not all) Muslim students feel stigmatised and that they need to self-censor as a result of Prevent. This corroborates the claims made by the NUS, Muslim lobby groups and others that the Prevent Duty, combined with prejudice on campus, has served to marginalise Muslim students and staff in universities (Muslim Council of Britain, 2019; NUS, n.d.; University and College Union, 2015).

This also suggests a disconnection between the views of Muslim students and staff and the views of senior managers with responsibility for implementing the Duty. As shown in Chapter 3, our Prevent Lead interviewees were aware of claims that Prevent is placing censorial pressure on Muslims, but tended to doubt this was happening (at least on their own campus).

Conclusion

The evidence from these surveys shows that students strongly value the principle of freedom of speech (in contrast to popular stereotypes) – but also that they often see guarded liberal anti-discrimination measures as more important than unlimited speech. Students may not see these positions as contradictory; they may see such measures as necessary for certain situations, for example, redressing power imbalances between speakers, and for ensuring that vulnerable groups feel comfortable joining debates.

The increasing polarisation on campus about these issues is exacerbated by external agitators. Organisations like *Spiked* and HJS push students towards the extremes of libertarianism and no-platforming, respectively. More widely, they drive the binary narrative of moral panic about universities and students, presenting them as either manifestly dangerous (HJS) or stupidly restrictive (*Spiked*). Right-wing populists sneak into the gap between these claims; they point to both as evidence that academics and students are part of an 'elite' and do not have 'the people's' interests at heart. It becomes irrelevant that these narratives are false and largely the invention of those not on campus.

The university sector has tended to ignore the claims from such organisations and from populists, rather than debunking them in a coordinated, public way. This is a mistake that has damaged the sector's reputation. Our evidence shows there is ample reason to challenge the claims and their flawed methodologies directly.

We have also seen that a minority of students feel unable to express their views on campus as freely as they wish to. The scale of the problem is not as great as suggested by *Spiked*, but it is concerning nonetheless. Sometimes students with right-wing, socially conservative or pro-Israel views self-censor out of fear of criticism from others. The polarised public discourse is even reflected in the framing of some surveys of student opinion about freedom of speech. As with the HEPI survey (Hillman, 2016), survey respondents are asked simply whether they think there should be more or less freedom, and are not actively encouraged, for example, to consider the value of different approaches, like those of Mill and Hankinson Nelson, who advocate group discussion of divisive issues, or of Butler, who encourages challenging hate speech. Academics need to be encouraged to do more to tackle student risk aversion with positive group work; as explained in Chapter 7, they can foster approaches such as CofI pedagogy to facilitate free debate about divisive issues.

But students being risk-averse out of fear of criticism is only part of the problem. There is now clear evidence showing that the Prevent Duty is having a chilling effect on the freedom of speech of some Muslim students and staff, damaging trust between students and tutors. Moreover, the *Re/presenting Islam on Campus* evidence suggests that Prevent can both sustain negative stereotypes about Muslims and inhibit critical scrutiny of such stereotypes, by discouraging students from speaking as freely as they wish to in these debates. Perhaps most concerning are two cumulative findings: first, the ignorance of many staff and students about Prevent is clear evidence that they were neither consulted nor informed about this national programme, suggesting a democratic deficit. Second, those students and staff who do become concerned find that their views cannot be given a fair hearing: the *Re/presenting Islam on Campus* research team found that usually, the only channel open for students to raise concerns about Prevent is through the Prevent team itself, which complainants avoid for fear of inviting unwarranted scrutiny. The lack of neutral opportunities for discussing Prevent commits a testimonial injustice against those with views critical of it, and it disenfranchises them.

The Prevent Duty is not the only regulatory structure that shapes free speech issues on campus. In the following two chapters, we examine the impact of another factor – students' unions' status as charities, and their regulation by the Charity Commission.

References

Bennett, R. (2017) 'Universities Told They Must Protect Freedom of Speech', *The Sunday Times*, 21 March. https://www.thetimes.co.uk/article/universities-told-they-must-protect-freedom-of-speech-fzqhx7vqt.

Bokhari, A. (2020) 'Conservative Henry Jackson Society Includes Anti-Sharia Campaigners in "Extremism" Report', *Breitbart*, 24 January. https://www.breitbart.com/tech/2020/01/24/conservative-henry-jackson-society-includes-anti-sharia-campaigners-in-extremism-report/.

Bridge Initiative Team (2018) 'Factsheet: Henry Jackson Society', *Bridge*, 13 June. https://bridge.georgetown.edu/research/factsheet-henry-jackson-society/

Brown, K.E. and Saeed, T. (2015) 'Radicalization and Counter-radicalization at British Universities: Muslim Encounters and Alternatives', *Ethnic and Racial Studies*, 38, 11: 1952–1968. https://www.tandfonline.com/doi/full/10.1080/01419870.2014.911343.

Department for Business, Innovation and Skills, Home Office, Prime Minister's Office, The Right Hon David Cameron and The Right Hon Jo Johnson (2015) 'PM's Extremism Taskforce: Tackling Extremism in Universities and Colleges Top of the Agenda'. Press release, 17 September. https://www.gov.uk/government/news/pms-extremism-taskforce-tackling-extremism-in-universities-and-colleges-top-of-the-agenda.

Ehsan, R. and Stott, P. (2020a) *Far-Right Terrorist Manifestos: A Critical Analysis*. London: The Henry Jackson Society. https://henryjacksonsociety.org/wp-content/uploads/2020/02/HJS-Terrorist-Manifesto-Report-WEB.pdf.

Ehsan, R. and Stott, P. (eds.) (2020b) *Countering the Far-Right: An Anthology*. London: The Henry Jackson Society. https://henryjacksonsociety.org/wp-content/uploads/2020/04/HJS-Far-Right-Anthology-Report-web.pdf.

Fox, E. (2019a) 'Extreme Speakers and Events: In the 2017–18 Academic Year'. *Henry Jackson Society*, 21 January. https://henryjacksonsociety.org/publications/university-extreme-speakers-2017-18-edition/.

Fox, E. (2019b) *Extreme Speakers and Events: In the 2017/18 Academic Year*. London: Henry Jackson Society. https://henryjacksonsociety.org/wp-content/uploads/2019/10/HJS-Extreme-Speakers-and-Events-Report.pdf.

Gilligan, A. (2019) 'Universities Double Invitations to Extremists', *The Sunday Times*, 20 January. https://www.thetimes.co.uk/article/universities-double-invitations-to-extremists-nxbg7fdwp.

Grant, J., Hewlett, K., Nir, T. and Duffy, R. (2019) *Freedom of Expression in UK Universities*. London: The Policy Institute, King's College London. https://www.kcl.ac.uk/policy-institute/assets/freedom-of-expression-in-uk-universities.pdf.

Guest, M., Aune, K., Sharma S. and Warner, R. (2013) *Christianity and the University Experience: Understanding Student Faith*. London: Bloomsbury.

Guest, M., Scott-Baumann, A., Cheruvallil-Contractor, S., Naguib, S., Phoenix, A., Lee, Y. and Al Baghal, T. (2020) *Islam and Muslims on UK University Campuses: Perceptions and Challenges*. Durham: Durham University, London: SOAS, Coventry: Coventry University and Lancaster: Lancaster University. https://www.soas.ac.uk/representingislamoncampus/publications/file148310.pdf.

Hillman, N. (2016) *Keeping Schtum? What Students Think of Free Speech*. HEPI Report no. 85. Oxford: Higher Education Policy Institute. https://www.hepi.ac.uk/wp-content/uploads/2016/05/.

Home Office (2011) *Prevent Strategy*. House of Commons Cm 8092. London: The Stationery Office. https://www.gov.uk/government/publications/prevent-strategy-2011.

Kassam, R. (2017) *No Go Zones: How Sharia Law Is Coming to a Neighbourhood Near You*. Washington, DC: Regnery Publishing.

Luke, C. (1994) 'Women in the Academy: The Politics of Speech and Silence', *British Journal of Sociology of Education*, 15: 2, 211–230. https://doi.org/10.1080/0142569940150204.

Mahmood, S. (2005) *Politics of Piety: The Islamic Revival and the Feminist Subject*. Princeton, NJ: Princeton University Press.

Murray, D. (2017) *The Strange Death of Europe: Immigration, Identity, Islam*. London: Continuum.

Muslim Council of Britain (2019) 'Muslim Council of Britain Responds to Prevent Review Legal Challenge'. Press release, 20 December. https://mcb.org.uk/press-releases/mcb-responds-to-prevent-review-legal-challenge/.

Naguib, S. (2020) 'Multiple Hierarchies: The Politics of Knowledge in Islamic Studies'. In Scott-Baumann, A., Guest, M., Naguib, S., Cheruvallil-Contractor, S., Phoenix, A., Al Baghal, T. and Lee, Y. *Islam on Campus: Contested Identities and the Cultures of Higher Education in Britain*. Oxford: Oxford University Press.

National Union of Students (2018) *The Experience of Jewish Students in 2017–18*. London: NUS. https://www.nusconnect.org.uk/resources/the-experience-of-muslim-students-in-2017-18.

National Union of Students (n.d.) 'Preventing Prevent'. www.nusconnect.org.uk/campaigns/preventing-prevent-we-are-students-not-suspects.

Nielsen, J.S. (2000) 'The Contribution of Interfaith Dialogue Towards a Culture of Peace', *Current Dialogue*, 36, December. https://sedosmission.org/old/eng/Nielsen.htm.

Office for Students (2019) *Prevent Monitoring Accountability and Data Returns 2017–18: Evaluation Report*. London: Office for Students. https://www.officeforstudents.org.uk/media/860e26e2-63e7-47eb-84e0-49100788009c/ofs2019_22.pdf.

Payne, S. (2015) 'Raheem Kassam Un-sacked as Nigel Farage's Senior Adviser', *The Spectator*, 14 May. https://www.spectator.co.uk/article/raheem-kassam-un-sacked-as-nigel-farage-s-senior-adviser.

Perfect, S., Aune, K. and Ryan, B. (2019) *Faith and Belief on Campus: Division and Cohesion. Exploring Student Faith and Belief Societies*. London: Theos. https://www.theosthinktank.co.uk/cmsfiles/Reportfiles/Theos---Faith-and-Belief-on-Campus---Division-and-Cohesion.pdf.

Perfect, S. with Scott-Baumann, A. (2019) 'A Critical Analysis of the Henry Jackson Society's Report *Extreme Speakers and Events: In the 2017/18 Academic Year*', SOAS. https://blogs.soas.ac.uk/cop/wp-content/uploads/2020/05/A-critical-analysis-of-the-Henry-Jackson-Society%E2%80%99s-report-Extreme-Speakers-and-Events.pdf.

Phoenix, A. (2020) 'Islam and Gender on Campus'. In Scott-Baumann, A., Guest, M., Naguib, S., Cheruvallil-Contractor, S., Phoenix, A., Al Baghal, T. and Lee, Y. *Islam on Campus: Contested Identities and the Cultures of Higher Education in Britain*. Oxford: Oxford University Press.

Saeed, T. (2019) 'Islamophobia and the Muslim Student: Disciplining the Intellect'. In Zempi, I. and Awan, I. (eds.) *The Routledge International Handbook on Islamophobia*. London: Routledge: 175–187.

Scott-Baumann, A., Guest, M., Naguib, S., Cheruvallil-Contractor, S., Phoenix, A., Al Baghal, T. and Lee, Y. (2020) *Islam on Campus: Contested Identities and the Cultures of Higher Education in Britain*. Oxford: Oxford University Press.

Simcox, R., Stuart, H., Ahmed, H. and Murray, D. (2011) *Islamist Terrorism: The British Connections*. 2nd ed. London: The Henry Jackson Society. http://henryjacksonsociety.org/wp-content/uploads/2011/07/Islamist+Terrorism+2011+Preview-1.pdf.

Slater, T. (2019) 'Free Speech University Rankings', *Spiked Online*, 24 February. https://www.spiked-online.com/free-speech-university-rankings/

Sorial, S. (2012) *Sedition and the Advocacy of Violence: Free Speech and Counter-Terrorism*. London: Routledge.

Spiked Online (2018) *Free Speech University Rankings 2018*. https://media.spiked-online.com/website/images/2019/02/21153835/FSUR-PACK-2018.pdf.

Stewart, H. and Mason, R. (2016) 'Nigel Farage's Anti-migrant Poster Reported to Police', *The Guardian*, 16 June. https://www.theguardian.com/politics/2016/jun/16/nigel-farage-defends-ukip-breaking-point-poster-queue-of-migrants.

Telis, N., Glassberg, E.C., Pritchard, J.K. and Gunter, C. (2019) 'Public Discussion Affects Question Asking at Academic Conferences', *The American Journal of Human Genetics*, 105, 2: 189–197. https://doi.org/10.1016/j.ajhg.2019.06.004.

Thompson, C. (2018) 'Free Speech Infringements on British Campuses: A Genuine Crisis – or Fake News and Fabrication?' In Joint Committee on Human Rights (2018) *Freedom of Speech in Universities*. Written evidence, FSU0011. http://data.parliament.uk/WrittenEvidence/CommitteeEvidence.svc/EvidenceDocument/Human%20Rights%20Joint%20Committee/Freedom%20of%20Speech%20in%20Universities/written/75393.html.

University and College Union (2015) 'The Prevent Duty: A Guide for Branches and Members', December. https://www.ucu.org.uk/media/7370/The-prevent-duty-guidance-for-branches-Dec-15/pdf/ucu_preventdutyguidance_dec15.pdf.

Usmani, M.T. (2013) 'Slavery in Islam', *Deoband*, 26 January. Translated by Zameelur Rahman. https://www.deoband.org/2013/01/hadith/hadith-commentary/slavery-in-islam/

Waldron, J. (2012) *The Harm in Hate Speech*. Cambridge, MA: Harvard University Press.

5 Charity law, political activism and speaking freely in students' unions

From organising soup kitchens to raising money for charity, students' unions are powerful drivers of social action. The scale of their charitable giving is huge: in 2016/17, for example, 39 unions raised nearly £2.75 million for charity between them (National Student Fundraising Association, 2017). This work is facilitated by the unions' legal status as charities, which brings them benefits, including tax relief. But charitable status comes at a price – unions face restrictions on political activism. This is a crucial, but often overlooked, factor shaping freedom of speech on campus.

In this chapter, we explore the impact of charity law and charitable status on free speech and political activism in students' unions since 2010. We pay particular attention to the impact on Muslim students. Our focus is on unions regulated by the Charity Commission for England and Wales. We draw on our empirical research, including interviews with 20 chief executive officers (CEOs) and sabbatical officers[1] from a range of students' unions, conducted in 2016–17.

As part of our analysis, we draw on the work of two public intellectuals and philosophers – the American Stanley Fish and the Frenchman Paul Ricoeur – to answer the question: is it right that students' unions should face restrictions on their activities?

From exempt to regulated charities

Underpinning the idea of charity is the aspiration towards a common good, yet also the inability of liberal democratic politics to be just to all. Thus, from a philosophical perspective, charity and politics are indivisible. Yet in English law, there is a longstanding principle that charities cannot spend supporters' money on activities not directly related to their aims – and in particular, on 'political activity'. This is defined by the Charity Commission as, for example, furthering the interests of a political party, or securing or opposing a particular change in the law (Charity Commission, 2019: OG 48, Section 6.2).

Students' unions have been charities, subject to charity law, for decades. In the 1970s and 1980s, a number of court cases arose after unions tried to donate money to various causes, such as to striking miners. These cases, and the Education Act 1994, confirmed that students' unions are educational charities independent from their parent universities and cannot use their resources in ways that do not further their formal charitable purposes (also known as the 'charitable objects') (Farrington and Palfreyman, 2012: 218–224).

Until the late 2000s, most students' unions had 'exempt charity status', meaning they were regulated only by their parent universities, and not by the Charity Commission. They lost this exempt status with the passing of the Charities Act 2006, which among other things sought to strengthen accountability in exempt charities, including students' unions. When HEFCE (the regulator of English universities between 1992 and 2018) declined to become the regulator of students' unions for charity purposes, the Charity Commission stepped in. Unions were required to register with the Commission by 2010 if they had a gross annual income of over £100,000 (Day and Dickinson, 2018: 45; Charity Commission, 2019: OG 48, Section 2).

This represented a dramatic change. Faced with a new and powerful regulator, which could sanction them for non-compliance, after 2010 students' unions were forced to refocus on their legal obligations as charities. Most improved their governance and accountability structures (Day and Dickinson, 2018: 45–46). Crucially, they also had to pay renewed attention to the restrictions on freedom of speech and action embedded within recent charity law.

Charity law implications for students' unions

The legal restrictions on what charities can do and say reflects the idea that they must be politically 'neutral' and avoid party politics. While these restrictions are unproblematic for most charities, they sit in tension with some of the common activities of students' unions. Charities cannot devote substantial resources to 'political activity'; they are allowed to campaign on and make corporate statements about national or international issues – but only if those activities are 'legitimate' and 'reasonable' means of furthering their charitable objects (Charity Commission, 2019: OG 48, Section 6.3). For most students' unions, these objects are usually concerned with advancing students' education and welfare.

For some, the restriction on students' unions devoting resources to political activity is welcome because they believe that universities should stay out of politics. Fish sums up this approach:

> The university that rigorously distances itself from politics will at once be true to its mission and more likely to prosper politically.
> (Fish, 2019: 87)

His advice to universities to keep away from politics seems to relate to his belief that the campus is separate from 'the world':

> Politics as an activity exists because the default condition of human beings is not agreement but difference. Each of us has a different understanding of what the world is like and of what should be done to improve it.
> (Fish, 2019: 176)

For Fish, however, universities are not to be involved in advocating for particular positions in political debate. UK charity law enforces this position. This begs the question of what is political and what is not, and what the purpose of Higher Education might be.

How, then, do students' unions determine whether particular activities are allowed under charity law, or whether they are 'ultra vires' ('beyond the powers') and thus impermissible? This can be a difficult area. In its original 2010 guidance for students' unions (which was revised in November 2018), the Charity Commission said it would consider it acceptable for students' unions to comment publicly on issues such as 'street lighting near the campus' or 'more public transport' to campus at night. It would be unacceptable, however, for them to issue statements on issues that (in the Commission's view) 'do not affect the welfare of students *as students* [emphasis added]' – such as 'campaigns to outlaw the killing of whales' or 'the treatment of political prisoners in a foreign country' (cited in JCHR, 2018: 34; McCall and Desai, 2016: 5). The thrust of this seems to be in line with Fish's ideas and runs counter to a common expectation that students' unions *should* be hubs of campaigning and debate on challenging political issues, including ones that affect the general population, not just students 'as students'. It seems strange that students' unions should be told they can comment on street lights but not important global issues that their students care about.

We raised this point in our submissions to the 2017 Joint Committee on Human Rights' (JCHR) inquiry into freedom of speech on campus. The MPs agreed with our criticisms, finding that the Commission's guidance was problematic and created 'confusion around what student[s'] unions feel they can comment on' (JCHR, 2018: 34). As a result, the Commission has now removed these specific examples from its guidance. Nonetheless, students' unions are still expected to avoid political activity or making corporate statements that do not clearly further their charitable objects (Charity Commission, 2019: OG 48 Sections 6.2–6.3; McCall and Desai, 2016: 4–11).

Charity trustees are also required to protect their organisation from abuse for extreme or terrorist purposes. Guidance from the Commission states that charities would breach charity law if they promote 'extremist views', even if these 'are not violent or not likely to incite violence', and even when their expression falls 'well below the criminal threshold'. The guidance notes that extreme views include those that 'are harmful to social cohesion', such as denigrating people of a particular faith or promoting segregation on religious grounds. Moreover, charities can host people with 'controversial views', but only if this is compatible with the trustees' legal duties – including avoiding putting the charity's reputation at undue risk and ensuring that the charities' activities are 'for the public benefit'. The guidance is a warning: it states that the promotion by charities of extreme or controversial (but lawful) views may fail this public benefit requirement (Charity Commission, 2018b: Section 5.2).

These rules have important implications for free speech. The Prevent Duty focuses on extreme views that may lead a person into terrorism. The Charity Commission's guidance, however, expands the categorisation of views to be considered problematic beyond the ambiguous realm of 'extremism' to the even more ill-defined realm of 'controversy'. Thus charities are told to be cautious about, or even to avoid, hosting views that, though controversial, 'might fall well below the criminal threshold' (Charity Commission, 2018b: Section 5.2). In Chapter 6 we show the direct interaction between charity rules and Prevent via the Charity Commission's interventions on campus.

These rules are particularly relevant for students' unions. They are much more likely than most other charities to host speakers with 'controversial' views because their societies often wish to explore a range of viewpoints. The Commission guidance encourages unions towards risk aversion when it comes to engaging in political activity or hosting speakers with divisive views. This pushes them in the opposite direction from their parent universities, which are required to uphold freedom of speech as far as 'reasonably practicable', including for people with offensive views (Education (No. 2) Act 1986, s. 43). The Prevent Duty, which applies to universities (and not their students' unions), requires them to pay 'particular regard' to their free speech requirements while fulfilling the Duty; in contrast, the original Charity Commission guidance had no such expectation that students' unions should consider freedom of speech when dealing with speaker events (Attle, 2018).

Following the JCHR's scrutiny, the Commission's revised guidance now clarifies that students' unions can host debates on issues that may be considered 'political, controversial ... unpopular or provocative', and that freedom of speech 'should form part of the fundamental consideration' when they are carrying out their activities (Charity Commission, 2019: OG 48, Section 7.1). But how exactly this fits with the rest of the guidance, including the need to avoid bringing the charity's reputation into undue risk, is unclear. Overall, the weight of charity law and guidance still encourages students' unions towards no-platforming as a default position for controversial speakers.

Political activism within students' unions

We explored the practical implications of the re-emphasis (after 2010) on the status of students' unions as charities in our research with union CEOs and sabbatical officers. Many of the CEOs had been involved in registering their unions with the Charity Commission, so had seen first-hand the impact on their union. Overall, most said that despite the change, their union staff were able to carry out their activities as they wished, including political activism and campaigning. But they had to be more careful in how they documented decision making, presenting campaigning activities as benefitting students 'as students' specifically, rather than the general population.

In contrast, in some unions the re-emphasis on charity status has had a detrimental impact on how free their staff and officers feel they are to engage in political activism. One CEO described charity status as 'clipping our wings' in terms of his union's activities and freedom of speech:

> In principle, [charity] requirements are good – we've got to be fair, balanced, democratic. But it has stopped allowing SUs to express themselves in full about geopolitical situations ... [It is affecting] what we can and cannot talk about, what we can and cannot campaign nationally on.

He said that charity regulations had made him regrettably 'risk-averse' when considering student requests for support in campaigning, or for potentially controversial speakers. He was particularly wary because the Charity Commission had scrutinised his union after the media reported that a former student had become radicalised (after he had left university) and joined ISIS:

> I say 'no' more often than 'yes' these days, it's disappointing. I didn't join students' unions to prevent students from doing things.

For him, adhering to charity law meant avoiding any risk to his union's reputation, which meant avoiding activity that might be perceived by the media as controversial. He felt he had to adopt guarded liberalism as the union's default approach to freedom of speech, and no-platforming for controversial speakers.

Other interviewees similarly thought that the increased focus on unions' charitable status had encouraged a culture of risk aversion:

> This creates a culture among sabbaticals of, 'oh, I assume I can't do this' [under charity rules].

It seems that some unions are being squeezed into Fish's position that universities should avoid politics and controversy and 'stick to their academic knitting' (Fish, 2019: 87). Some union staff now view freedom of speech solely as a dangerous risk to be managed – the second contemporary trend we highlighted in the Introduction.

According to our interviewees, 'politically activist' sabbatical officers sometimes feel 'really constrained' by charity law restrictions. They have competing responsibilities – their legal ones as charity trustees, and their democratic ones as elected representatives of students. Our research found that some officers think these responsibilities are in tension, and feel frustrated that, as charity trustees, they cannot speak or act as boldly on political matters as their students might like. Thus freedom of speech as a value is discouraged by charity law: often the only debate that happens within unions is to clarify risk assessment and permissibility.

It can be difficult for students' unions to determine whether or not particular activities are permissible under charity rules. We heard about numerous cases where union staff and officers had difficult discussions about particular activities. Some had debated whether sabbatical officers could make political statements on their personal social media. In others, staff disagreed about whether they could issue formal public statements, as voted on by their student body, favouring particular political positions, such as in support of striking junior doctors in 2016 or the Remain campaign in the EU Referendum. There has been a 'charitisation' and 'legalisation' of discourse around activism within students' unions, where both sides in a debate make appeals to charity law to support their competing positions. Students in one union passed a motion calling for it to advocate for remaining in the EU in 2016, but the union's trustee board vetoed the motion out of concern that it would transgress charity law. Some of the union staff thought the trustees had interpreted charity rules in an overly risk-averse way. They were frustrated that the union was unable to take a public position even though their parent university had done so.

In their regulatory interactions with students' unions, Charity Commission officers have sometimes discouraged them from campaigning on national issues. Arguably, students' unions should be able to campaign in support of striking junior doctors, or against cuts to the NHS, for example, because these issues affect the interests of students as much as anyone else. Yet one CEO said that, during an audit of her union, Commission officers had cited these as examples of topics they would consider it inappropriate for unions to campaign on, unless it could be shown clearly that the campaigns were restricted to issues that specifically affect students 'as students', not students as general citizens. Fish would presumably find this a useful distinction; we find it counterproductive.

Activism related to Israel/Palestine seems particularly likely to lead to fraught discussions among students' union staff – especially the Boycott, Divestment and Sanctions (BDS) movement against Israel. Small activities can lead to big debates: one CEO said his union spent a 'ridiculous' amount of time debating whether it was permissible under charity rules for staff to put up a poster in their office supporting the boycott. In some universities, students voted to commit their unions formally to supporting BDS; while some students' unions obliged, in others the trustee boards vetoed the motions due to concerns about charity rules. In fact, the Charity Commission has confirmed it would most likely consider attempts to support BDS as going beyond a union's charitable objects, thereby breaching the rules (Charity Commission, 2018a: 4). The Conservative government may seek to prohibit public bodies from supporting BDS over the next few years, as indicated in its 2019 manifesto (Conservative and Unionist Party, 2019).

Some university students and staff see current charity rules as dampening free speech on the BDS movement, and on Israel/Palestine more widely – as one sabbatical officer told us, 'there is frustration' among some students 'that the SU can't take stances on Israel and

Palestine'. But conversely, it can be argued that BDS itself undermines freedom of speech on campus, by discouraging those who support Israel's policies from expressing their views. Indeed, an NUS survey of 485 Jewish students in 2016–17 found that half felt uncomfortable engaging in debate on Israel/Palestine on campus, with some feeling that their unions' BDS policies increased hostility towards Jews (National Union of Students, 2017: 25–26). This situation shows the complexity of navigating freedom of speech issues on campus regarding Israel/Palestine issues. Both supporters and opponents of BDS can justify their arguments by appealing to freedom of speech.

University staff can find it difficult to make judgement calls between these competing claims. An innovative solution is the emergence of student societies that seek to create a setting for conversations and friendships between people with opposing views on this issue – one example being the Voices of Israel–Palestine established at the London School of Economics in 2017 (Reiff, 2019).

As we have seen, sometimes these discussions about political activism end with union trustee boards deciding that charity law prohibits them from implementing decisions voted for by students. Thus a students' union's status as a charity can conflict with its status as a democratic body representing students' interests. Some of our CEO interviewees were worried about this and sought to discourage students from submitting motions that might be difficult to enact under charity law (for example, motions that would require the union to commit funds to 'political' causes). This tactic of managing possible motions may help to maintain the appearance of democracy within a students' union (McCall and Desai, 2016: 10–11). However, arguably it amounts to a further constraining of freedom of speech, by limiting the range of decisions that students can make even before they submit motions.

Ultimately, it appears that a minority of sabbatical officers and students feel constrained by the restrictions of charity law on political activism; yet their concerns must still be taken seriously. They are often at universities with reputations for having especially 'politically active' student bodies or significant numbers of students from ethnic or religious minority backgrounds. Some interviewees felt there had been a depoliticisation of their student body recently – partly as a result of tuition fee rises forcing students to spend more time focusing on studying and earning money than on activism. If this depoliticisation is indeed happening, then it is a serious loss for Higher Education and for society more widely.

Handling external speakers

Many of our interviewees emphasised that their union took external speakers' freedom of speech very seriously. They differed, however, in how far they would go to uphold that freedom in practice. Some CEOs said they had never turned down a request for a speaker from students. Instead, they would put in place factors to mitigate any risks arising from hosting controversial speakers, such as ensuring the event was managed by an independent chair – a typical guarded liberal approach. In one case, a CEO said that her union was due to host a speaker who had previously 'expressed support for a proscribed organisation'; he would be hosted nonetheless because he was being invited to speak about an unrelated subject. In this instance, the union chose to adopt the liberal approach to freedom of speech, believing it more important to uphold that freedom than to follow the pressure from charity law to avoid controversy.

Other unions in our sample were less willing to host controversial speakers. A sabbatical officer said his organisation had twice turned down students' requests for Moazzam Begg (an example of no-platforming), out of concern about controversial comments he had made in the past, and a desire to protect students' 'welfare'. Begg is the Outreach Director of CAGE – an organisation that lobbies against what it calls 'repressive state policies' initiated under the War on Terror but which has faced repeated accusations of supporting extremism (CAGE, n.d.; McMicking, 2015). This union did host other speakers with potentially controversial views (such as the feminist Julie Bindel, who has faced accusations of transphobia) (Minou, 2010; Hope, 2017). But where the union staff thought the speaker might 'question the legitimacy of a minority group', they would 'require a disclaimer on the [event] advertisement ... that this isn't a safe space for students'. This is a guarded liberal approach, allowing speech to go ahead but only under certain limitations.

As we have seen, still other unions have been forced unwillingly into guarded liberalism and no-platforming as default (as opposed to one-off) positions, as a result of the renewed focus on their charitable status after 2010 and the introduction of the Prevent Duty in 2015. One CEO, feeling under pressure from the Charity Commission to avoid risks to his union's reputation, reluctantly sought to discourage students from requesting potentially controversial speakers:

> It's led to some speakers being talked about and being stopped before they're even presented as potential candidates.

The CEO admitted those speakers 'tend to be Muslim'. These were not necessarily people with unlawful or extreme views, but speakers reflecting the 'more conservative view of religion' shared (in his view) by many of the university's Muslim students. The union's worries about meeting its charitable duties meant that Muslim students were put at a clear disadvantage, being less able than others to invite the speakers they wanted. This chimes with our findings discussed in Chapter 4, that some Muslim students feel they need to avoid inviting potentially controversial speakers out of fear they may invite Prevent scrutiny upon themselves. In some unions Muslim risk aversion is exacerbated by union   media coverage and the threat of sanction by the Charity Commission.

Bureaucracy and the balance of power between universities and their unions

The emphasis on students' unions' charitable status from 2010 has also affected freedom of speech on campus in other, less direct ways.

One way is through increased bureaucracy in booking external speakers. Many unions updated their processes for vetting student requests for speakers, in order to align with the Charity Commission's guidance and (after 2015) with the Prevent Duty. In many, the process for securing a speaker has become more intensive, and according to the JCHR, sometimes this creates bureaucratic hurdles 'which could deter students from holding events and inviting external speakers' (Joint Committee on Human Rights, 2018: 37). According to one study of university freedom of speech codes, some universities and unions now require students to submit their speaker requests at least a month in advance of the planned event to allow time for them to be vetted (in other universities, the time required is as little as five days) (Beech, 2018: 21–22). In the compressed timescale of university life, a requirement that students submit their requests a month in advance can be difficult to meet – particularly if the intended speaker is a last-minute replacement for someone else, or a late addition to secure a balanced panel. This might mean that some events cannot go ahead, and some students might be deterred from organising speaker events at all.

Beyond this, as students' unions have refocused on their charitable status, the balance of power between them and their parent universities has changed, so that some now have less freedom to challenge university policies they consider unfair. Since the 1990s, many unions have focused less on raising money from commercial ventures and more on supporting the educational and welfare needs of their students, and from 2010 unions needed to focus on compliance with their educational charitable objects (Day and Dickinson, 2018: 44–45, 73). While this has benefited students in some ways, it has also made many unions heavily dependent upon the funding they receive from their parent university. This financial dependency may be of no consequence if relations between a union and its university are amicable. But some commentators have warned of a potential 'chilling effect' on unions' activism when they become reliant on their university's goodwill for funding (Parr, 2014). Some universities use this situation to exert greater control over their union, such as by requiring that university representatives sit on the union's trustee board in return for funding. In such scenarios, the capacity of students' unions to challenge their universities, or to undertake campaigns that the universities disapprove of, would be seriously inhibited.

Conclusion

The tightening of interpretation of charitable status by a proactive Charity Commission since 2010 has brought students' unions some benefits. In particular, they have been pushed to establish stronger governance structures, which have improved their financial management and long-term planning.

However, it is clear that in some unions, the loss of exempt charity status (by coming under the direct regulation of the Commission) has also made them risk-averse in their political activism and external speaker debates. Worried about the consequences if they fail to comply with charity law, they have been pushed, sometimes unwillingly, towards the guarded liberal approach to freedom of speech as a default setting – and in some cases, to no-platforming as a standard response to any proposed speakers who may be controversial. Sometimes students have been informally discouraged from even inviting certain speakers; such no-platforming would not be recorded in the data of the Office for Students (OfS) on university events (OfS, 2019: 10). In some universities this disproportionately disadvantages Muslim students (particularly those with socially conservative views), who find themselves less free than others to discuss the topics they want with the speakers they want.

This state of affairs has arisen because students' unions face a restrictive definition of politics, as something they should avoid. Fish's answer to whether it is right that students' unions should face restrictions on their activism would be a resounding *yes* on grounds that universities should keep away from politics.

By contrast, Ricoeur's answer would be *no*, because he insisted upon the importance of challenging ideologies underpinning systems of power, and he regretted the limitations caused by what he called political correctness, exemplified for him by McCarthyism in the United States. He believed that the 'harm produced by political correctness becomes obvious when certain forms of discourse are forbidden; then it is freedom of expression, the formal condition of free discussion, that is threatened' (Ricoeur, 1998: 56). He would see charity law's restrictions on students' unions' activism as preventing students from engaging in 'the critical spirit which rests on shared common rules of discussion' (Ricoeur, 1998: 56).

We agree with this view. As democratic institutions representing students, the unions should be organs through which students can engage in politics. While it is fair that students' unions should not be *party*-political (publicly endorsing a particular political party, which does not represent the interests of all students), we argue they should be able to campaign on, and devote resources to, major political issues that affect everyone, not just 'students as students'. For example, if students pass a motion to devote resources to campaigns protesting an economic policy (which is not unlikely as we face an economic crisis following COVID-19), we think their students' union should have at least the possibility of enacting the motion if they so wish. This would exemplify deliberative democracy: discussion, choices, voting and enactment. Yet under the current rules the union would most likely need to veto the motion without considering its merits.

Beyond the various effects of charitable status discussed here, the Charity Commission's intervention in the sector is also an important factor in shaping freedom of speech on campus. We turn to this in the next chapter.

Note

1 Sabbatical officers are elected, paid members of a students' union executive. They are usually students taking a year out of study, or are new graduates. They are also charity trustees for the union.

References

Attle, G. (2018) 'Supplementary Written Evidence from Gary Attle, Partner, Mills & Reeve LLP'. In Joint Committee on Human Rights (2018) *Freedom of Speech in Universities*. Written evidence, FSU0104. http://data.parliament.uk/WrittenEvidence/CommitteeEvidence.svc/EvidenceDocument/Human%20Rights%20Joint%20Committee/Freedom%20of%20Speech%20in%20Universities/written/78121.html.

Beech, D. (2018) *An Analysis of UK University Free Speech Policies Prepared for the Joint Committee for Human Rights*. London: Higher Education Policy Institute. https://www.parliament.uk/documents/joint-committees/human-rights/2015-20-parliament/HEPIreport090218.pdf.

CAGE (n.d.) 'About Us'. https://www.cage.ngo/about-us.

Charity Commission (2018a) 'Written Evidence from the Charity Commission for England and Wales'. In Joint Committee on Human Rights (2018) *Freedom of Speech in Universities*. Written evidence, FSU0093. http://data.parliament.uk/writtenevidence/committeeevidence.svc/evidencedocument/human-rights-committee/freedom-of-speech-in-universities/written/76814.pdf.

Charity Commission (2018b) *Protecting Charities from Abuse for Extremist Purposes*. https://www.gov.uk/government/publications/protecting-charities-from-abuse-for-extremist-purposes/chapter-5-protecting-charities-from-abuse-for-extremist-purposes.

Charity Commission (2019) *Charity Commission Operational Guidance*. OG 48, 'Students' Unions'. http://ogs.charitycommission.gov.uk/g048a001.aspx.

Conservative and Unionist Party (2019) *Get Brexit Done: Unleash Britain's Potential*. Party Manifesto. https://assets-global.website-files.com/5da42e2cae7ebd3f8bde353c/5dda924905da587992a064ba_Conservative%202019%20Manifesto.pdf.

Day, M. and Dickinson, J. (2018) *David versus Goliath: The Past, Present and Future of Students' Unions in the UK*. HEPI Report No. 111. London: Higher Education Policy Institute. https://www.hepi.ac.uk/wp-content/uploads/2018/09/HEPI-Students-Unions-Report-111-FINAL-EMBARGOED1.pdf.

Education (No. 2) Act 1986. https://www.legislation.gov.uk/ukpga/1986/61.

Farrington, D. and Palfreyman, D. (2012) *The Law of Higher Education*. 2nd ed. Oxford: Oxford University Press.

Fish, S. (2019) *The First: How to Think about Hate Speech, Campus Speech, Religious Speech, Fake News, Post-Truth, and Donald Trump*. New York: Atria/One Signal.

Hope, S. (2017) 'Julie Bindel's Transphobia Is a Constant Source of Trauma', *The Queerness*, 8 January. https://thequeerness.com/2017/01/08/julie-bindel-transphobia-source-trauma/.

Joint Committee on Human Rights (2018) *Freedom of Speech in Universities*. House of Lords/House of Commons (HC 589; HL Paper 111): Fourth Report of Session 2017–19. London: The Stationery Office. https://publications.parliament.uk/pa/jt201719/jtselect/jtrights/589/589.pdf.

McCall, C. and Desai, R. (2016) 'In the Matter of an Opinion for the National Union of Students'. http://www.uklfi.com/UKLFI%20-%20student%20anti-BDS%20guide/Opinion%20-%20Christopher%20McCall%20&%20Raj%20Desai.pdf.

McMicking, H. (2015) 'Cage: Important Human Rights Group or Apologists for Terror?', *BBC News*, 27 February. https://www.bbc.co.uk/news/uk-31657333.

Minou, C.L. (2010) 'Julie Bindel's dangerous transphobia', *The Guardian*, 1 February. https://www.theguardian.com/commentisfree/2010/feb/01/julie-bindel-transphobia.

National Student Fundraising Association (2017) '39 Student Unions Raise £2.7m for Charity', 4 December. https://www.nasfa.org.uk/articles/39-student-unions-raise-2-7m-for-charity.

National Union of Students (2017) *The Experience of Jewish Students in 2016–17*. London: NUS. https://www.nusconnect.org.uk/resources/The-experience-of-Jewish-students-in-2016-17.

Office for Students (2019) *Prevent Monitoring Accountability and Data Returns 2017–18: Evaluation Report*. London: Office for Students. https://www.officeforstudents.org.uk/media/860e26e2-63e7-47eb-84e0-49100788009c/ofs2019_22.pdf.

Parr, C. (2014) 'Off the Booze: Students' Unions Shift from Serving to Service', *Times Higher Education*, 17 April. https://www.timeshighereducation.com/features/off-the-booze-students-unions-shift-from-serving-to-service/2012658.article.

Reiff, B. (2019) 'Can the Israel–Palestine Campus War Become a Conversation?', *Haaretz*, 21 July. https://www.haaretz.com/world-news/.premium-can-the-israel-palestine-campus-war-become-a-conversation-1.7545514.

Ricoeur, P. (1998) *Critique and Conviction*. Translated by K. Blamey. Cambridge: Polity Press.

6 The Charity Commission's interventions in students' unions

The risk aversion affecting some students' unions is exacerbated by the direct intervention of the unions' regulator, the Charity Commission.

In this chapter, we examine the role of the Charity Commission for England and Wales, which gained authority over students' unions after the passing of the Charities Act 2006. As well as drawing on our interviews with chief executive officers (CEOs) of students' unions conducted in 2016–17, we analyse in detail the correspondence between one students' union and the Charity Commission in 2016–18.

Our research took place before the Commission updated its guidance (in response to the inquiry of the Joint Committee on Human Rights (JCHR)) to include an acknowledgement of the importance of freedom of speech for students' unions (Charity Commission, 2019: OG 48, Section 7.1). We show how, until then, the Commission had little concern for freedom of speech on campus. Its regulatory approach has risked undermining rigorous debate of difficult topics on campus, by encouraging unions to avoid not only 'extreme' but also 'controversial' speakers. When students are deprived of the facts and of the opportunity to debate, explore and question experts about complex matters in the manner they wish, this creates a democratic deficit. We subject the narratives of harm and controversy to scrutiny by comparing the Commission's interventions with the views of major thinkers, including Kant, Abou El Fadl and Sorial.

The Charity Commission's interest in extremism and students' unions

The Charity Commission's powers and ambitions have transformed in recent years. Between 2008 and 2018, its budget roughly halved in real terms (Cooney, 2016), and in 2013 it was criticised by the National Audit Office (NAO) for being ineffective at tackling 'abuse' in the charity sector (NAO, 2013). Pressure mounted as media stories emerged linking staff members of a number of charities – often Muslim ones – to supposed terrorist organisations (for example, Turner, 2014). In response, the government beefed up the Commission's powers substantially. In 2014, it received £8 million to help it prevent charitable money being used to fund extremist or terrorist activity (Cabinet Office et al., 2014), and in 2016 its powers to act against organisations suspected of such abuse were greatly enhanced (Charities (Protection and Social Investment) Act 2016). Thus it has become a much more prescriptive and proactive regulator, being particularly concerned to crack down on perceived extremism among charities.

This shift was driven by William Shawcross, the Commission's Chair between 2012 and 2018. The appointment of Shawcross, a writer, commentator and former board member of the Henry Jackson Society (HJS), caused controversy. Labour and Liberal Democrat members of Parliament's Public Administration Committee voted against it, arguing that his published support for the Conservative Party created a 'conflict of interest' (Holmes, 2014). He was also known to have made hostile, alarmist remarks about immigration, Islam and Muslims. In 2012, for example, in a speech on behalf of the HJS, he claimed that 'Europe and Islam is one of the greatest, most terrifying problems of our future' (Ramesh, 2014).

Under Shawcross' leadership, the Charity Commission faced accusations of a 'move toward the right' (ThirdSector, 2013) and lack of independence from the government (Kennedy and Ferrell-Schweppenstedde, 2018). In 2015, a report from the Panel on the Independence of the Voluntary Sector, established by the Baring Foundation, said the Commission was 'being politically driven' and 'sending ambiguous signals about the role of political campaigning which may well have a chilling effect' (Civil Exchange, 2015: 52). It was also accused of focusing disproportionately on Muslim charities (Pudelek, 2014; Delmar-Morgan, 2015), with one report claiming that such charities were the subject of 38% of all disclosed statutory investigations by the Commission between 1 January and 23 April 2014 (Mason, 2014).

One particularly high-profile case exemplified these concerns. In 2015, media outlets reported that charitable funds given to the controversial organisation CAGE[1] had been used to support Mohammed Emwazi, who later on was radicalised and became the notorious ISIS terrorist 'Jihadi John'. The Charity Commission sought to force CAGE's funders, including the Joseph Rowntree Charitable Trust (JRCT), to cease all present or future funding of CAGE, leading to a legal challenge – with the Commission ultimately accepting that it did not have the power to fetter charities' lawful discretion in who to fund in the future. During the hearing, the court was shown emails where the Charity Commission board, including Shawcross, and even a government minister, unfairly sought to influence the Commission's investigation – accusing CAGE of supporting terrorism (without substantiation) and pushing for the investigators to make an example of the JRCT (Cook, 2015; Ramesh, 2015).

In this climate, and particularly since the 2015 introduction of the Prevent Duty, the Charity Commission has taken an active interest in students' unions. In 2015 it audited a number of unions to assess charity law compliance in the sector, and in April 2017 it wrote to various unions that had voted to support the Boycott, Divestment and Sanctions (BDS) movement against Israel, warning them that campaigning for the boycott could exceed their charitable purposes and discriminate against some students (Ironmonger, 2017; Kay, 2017). The Charity Commission is particularly concerned about the governance of the students' unions, external speaker requests and the risks of extremism on campus. More formally, from 2016 to 2018, the Commission undertook compliance investigations into six unions regarding external speakers, finding shortfalls in their risk assessment processes (Charity Commission, 2018: 20).

Students' knowledge of the Charity Commission

The Charity Commission has clearly become a significant player on campus, and as we saw in Chapter 5, the need to comply with charity regulations has pushed some students' union staff into risk aversion. We wanted to find out if students know about the Commission's regulation of students' unions. The 2015–18 AHRC-funded *Re/presenting Islam on Campus* student survey asked 2,022 respondents to choose from a list the bodies they thought are involved in 'overseeing students' discussions of controversial issues' on campus, and which bodies they thought *should* be involved.[2]

As shown in Figure 6.1, over 90% of UK university students did not realise that the Charity Commission has oversight of students' unions, with only 8.7% indicating knowledge of this. However, nearly twice as many students (16.5%) thought that the Charity Commission *should* be involved, while 83.5% did not see the need for this.

The results suggest that students' awareness of the Commission's role in oversight is low. Exploring the intersection of the questions shows that those who were previously aware of the Commission's

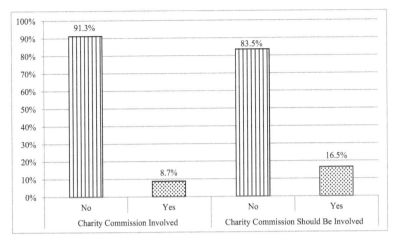

Figure 6.1 Full student sample knowledge of, and attitude towards, the Charity Commission's involvement in oversight of students' unions.

oversight were more likely than those who were not to think it should be involved. Those who were not aware may not have known about the Commission at all, or the charitable status of students' unions, and so may not have supported an unknown entity having oversight.

Dr Tarek Al Baghal of the University of Essex also analysed the responses of those students identifying as Muslims (247 respondents) in the AHRC-funded survey. Figure 6.2 shows similar responses to the whole sample. Muslims were slightly more aware of the Commission's involvement than students as a whole. However, they (and members of other religions) were significantly more likely to be aware than people with no religion.

Generally, however, Muslim awareness of the Commission's involvement is low. As with the low student awareness of the Prevent Duty, this suggests a democratic deficit, where students lack knowledge about structures that can inhibit what they say and do. Universities and students' unions have a responsibility to inform students about such issues.

Even more strikingly, when we gave evidence to the 2017 JCHR inquiry, it became clear that, like many students, the MPs did not know of the Charity Commission's involvement with students' unions as charities and the resultant impact on freedom of speech in certain cases. It was only after we (and others) referred to this in evidence that the JCHR decided to call the Charity Commission to give evidence.

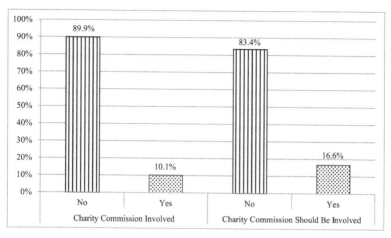

Figure 6.2 Muslim students' knowledge of, and attitude towards, the Charity Commission's involvement in oversight of students' unions.

Perceptions of the Charity Commission within the students' union sector

In our interview research, we asked the chief executive officers (CEOs) of students' unions about their impressions of the Charity Commission's regulation of the sector since 2010 (the year when unions were required to register with the Commission, having lost their exempt charity status under the Charities Act 2006). Our interviewees' responses were shaped both by their direct encounters with the Commission and by their political attitudes, including their views about external regulation and about how best to respond to 'extreme' views.

Most interviewees felt that the Commission was a light-touch regulator. Several found the Commission's advice helpful and said they had been motivated to ensure that their union had good governance structures in place.

Others, however, considered the Commission did not fully understand what students' unions aim to do and how they function. We were repeatedly informed that students' unions do not fit within the charity sector, in terms of their legal structures, as they are governed at least in part by student trustees elected each year rather than by highly experienced long-term appointments; their finances, as they are both welfare providers and trading organisations, and are often financially dependent upon their parent university; and – most importantly – their political activism.

Some of our interviewees were worried about the Charity Commission's approach to regulation, particularly its interest in extremism. Two CEOs whose unions had been selected for auditing by the Commission were concerned about the inspectors' interest in the Prevent Duty and the apparent risk of radicalisation among Islamic Societies. According to one interviewee:

> [The inspectors would say] 'you need to watch out for radicalisation' in the broadest sense and they'll chuck in some case studies which have never happened about BNP [British National Party] and animal rights and all the rest will be about ISocs [Islamic Societies] ... when they ask questions about societies which hold prayer events with external speakers, inevitably they're talking about ISocs.

Here, the Commission inspectors were primarily concerned about the risk of Muslim extremism rather than other kinds, and yet chose to avoid talking about this directly. Instead the conversation about extremism on campus could only be conducted through coded language and through an artificial attempt at maintaining 'balance'. We were told that at another union, during an audit by the Commission, the inspectors had presented screenshots of the Islamic Society's Facebook page, presumably because they were concerned about some of the Society's posts. Other societies' social media did not appear to be subject to such scrutiny. The CEO reporting this to us believed that the inspectors 'were only there for one purpose' – they had decided this union was a 'hotspot' for potential Islamist extremism. He also believed the regulator was trying to shape the boundaries of debate on campus, in a problematic way:

> The Charity Commission is now defining what is good or bad freedom of speech.

Some interviewees pointed out a connection between the Charity Commission and the Prevent Duty. The CEO of a London union said that Commission inspectors had asked him 'what are you doing to make sure that you are following the Prevent guidance?' The inspectors also advised that while unions are allowed to have a 'Preventing Prevent' policy on paper, in practice their charity law duty to protect students from harm means they must adhere to the Prevent Duty Guidance. This is striking because the Prevent Duty applies to university governing bodies but not students' union trustees. Despite this, the

Charity Commission has sought to push students' unions to comply with Prevent by presenting it as the only realistic way for charity trustees to meet their charity law requirements. We also saw this in the correspondence we analysed between the Commission and a particular students' union (discussed following).

Thus it appears that the Charity Commission sometimes acts as an informal Prevent enforcer, pushing students' unions to comply with it. In practice this is likely to increase such unions' risk aversion regarding external speakers still further. In Chapter 3 we used Strauss' 'persuasion principle' to show why Prevent's restrictions on lawful speech should be seen as wrong, because they interfere unduly with the listeners' and speakers' autonomy in the anticipation (without evidence) that controversial speakers will lead to radicalisation (Strauss, 1991). With the Charity Commission invoking Prevent, we can make the same judgment here. This also resonates with Kant's unconditional condemnation of lying, because lying is one manifestation of suppressed discussion (Kant, 2002).

Case study: investigation of a students' union's Palestine and Islamic Societies

The following case study explores the Charity Commission's investigation of a students' union from late 2016 to mid-2018. The Commission instigated a regulatory compliance case out of concern about the union's Palestine and Islamic Societies. The union has a reputation for being highly 'politically active', and less than half of the student body are white (Gamsu and Donnelly, 2017: Appendix Table 1).

We analyse the correspondence between the organisations, showing how the Charity Commission constructs and enforces its conception of 'extremism' in the students' union sector, and the impact of this on freedom of speech.

Outline of events

In late 2016, a newspaper reported that at an event about the Israel–Palestine conflict held by the students' union's Palestine Society, an external speaker expressed anti-Semitic views and conspiracy theories that were not challenged. A Charity Commission officer wrote to the union's trustees, asking them to explain why they thought this event furthered the charity's objects and was for the public benefit,[3] and to provide evidence of a risk assessment and a policy for vetting external speakers. The Commission officer said that the concerns raised by the newspaper may have led to a detrimental impact on public trust in both the charity and the charity sector in general.

In their response, the union trustees accepted there had been failings on their part: the Palestine Society had not confirmed the speaker's name in the room booking form and had not sufficiently challenged the speaker's statements during the event. Furthermore, the Question and Answer session was disrupted aggressively by non-students. Nonetheless, the trustees confirmed that they had since checked the speaker's views online and found nothing that would have indicated he was a cause for concern prior to the event. This did not, however, satisfy the Commission officer, who noted with concern the lack of robust vetting of the speaker and the absence of 'constructive challenge' to him.

Further, he argued that whilst the union could hold events where speakers challenge the policies of Israel, for an event to be 'educational', and so to fulfil the charity's objects, 'it must ensure balance and that opposing views and opinions are expressed so that those in attendance can make up their own minds'. This disregards the educational value of speech that is not 'balanced'. It reflects the Prevent Duty Guidance on handling speakers (Home Office, 2019: 11), but students' unions are not bound to follow this; moreover, as Scott-Baumann and Hugh Tomlinson QC, a specialist in freedom of expression law, point out, there is no legal requirement on universities to provide opposing voices:

> [I]f the speaker is going to stay within the law then the event must be allowed to proceed, even if there is no opposing speaker.
> (Scott-Baumann and Tomlinson, 2016)

Over several months, the Charity Commission contacted the students' union about three other incidents involving its Palestine or Islamic Societies, having become aware of these cases through media reports or by monitoring the societies' social media pages. In one case, the Commission was concerned that the Islamic Society was due to host a scholar who allegedly had made hateful comments against Jews, Shi'a Muslims and Christians in the past. The union trustees were asked to explain why they considered him a 'legitimate speaker'. In response, the trustees said the Islamic Society had not flagged the speaker on the room booking form as controversial, so the union had not undertaken an independent evaluation of him beyond the society's own risk assessment form. Upon receiving the Commission's correspondence, the trustees researched the speaker online, finding one article alleging that he had in the past made anti-Shi'a comments, and others where he apologised for offensive comments that he had made 15 years previously. The union trustees said they were satisfied that the speaker had sufficiently apologised for his past statements and so remained happy to have allowed the event to go ahead. They expressed confusion about why the Commission appeared to consider it inappropriate for the union to host him. But the trustees' response did not satisfy the Commission, which noted that a simple internet search revealed reports of the 'controversial statements' linked to the speaker.

This shows the tension that can arise between the distinct legal duties on universities and students' unions. As Scott-Baumann and Tomlinson (2016) point out, universities 'would be acting illegally if they refused a platform to speakers whose actions were unlikely to break the law' – such as the speaker in this example. But students' unions must adhere to charity law requirements to protect their reputation, and guidance from the Charity Commission – which in this case clearly did not think the union should have hosted the speaker.

Overall, the Charity Commission concluded that there were significant shortfalls in the union's administration, including insufficiently robust vetting procedures. It contacted the union again several months later, asking the trustees to demonstrate how they had improved their management of external speakers and to send a list of all events and speakers held by the Palestine and Islamic Societies in the intervening period. The trustees provided this evidence, including details of a revised room booking policy. However, the Commission found much of this evidence inadequate. It expressed surprise that the union had assessed the Palestine and Islamic Societies' speakers as being of low or medium risk and argued that the information given for some speakers was too vague for proper risk assessment. Consequently, the Commission concluded that the union seemed unable to assess the correct risk posed by controversial speakers. After the exchange of several letters, in which the students' union cited the importance of freedom of speech, the Commission ruled that the union was only 'partially compliant' with charity law. Then it closed the case.

Analysis

This case study shows the difficulties that students' unions can face when managing external speaker requests. The union was found to have failed to carry out adequate vetting of proposed speakers, in one case because it had accepted without question a student society's assessment of the level of risk. Following the Charity Commission's engagement, the union made various improvements to its room booking and risk assessment procedures, though it commented that the changes had doubled the time union staff needed to process room bookings.

The case study raises concerns about the Charity Commission's approach regarding students' unions and freedom of speech in the charity sector more widely. In Chapter 5 we showed that the Commission's guidance expands the range of views to be considered problematic from 'extremism', defined by the government as opposition to fundamental British values (Home Office, 2011: 107), to mere 'controversy'. What is meant by controversy is unclear, and thus it seems unreasonable to expect charities to be able to determine which perfectly legal (though undesirable) views should be avoided to satisfy the Charity Commission.

This use of the 'controversy' reason to suppress undesired views stops debate in its tracks. Alternatively, Abou El Fadl asserts that it is vital to debate publicly, not suppress, 'extreme' interpretations of Islam, and replace them with regionally appropriate versions of Islamic law – for example, through training imams within the United Kingdom with the full interplay of religious, secular and socio-economic expertise available in the universities and Muslim colleges. This would require changes in the British education system and the securitisation regime in order to support young British Muslims (Mukadam et al., 2010; Slater, 2018).

Our case study shows how this suppression operates in practice among students' unions. The Charity Commission is willing to use a charity's purposes, the public benefit requirement, and appeals to the charity's reputation, to discourage charities from hosting speakers with views it considers to be 'controversial'. It is striking that the Commission officer was sceptical that hosting controversial speakers could fulfil the union's educational purposes or be for the public benefit.

The Commission's position here resembles Sorial's position that extreme speech is not for the public benefit and should be discouraged. Sorial believes that universities have a ('negative') duty to exclude and delegitimise extremists, such as by denying them a platform (Sorial, 2012: 165). We agree with her that not all views have equal social value. Nonetheless, we are convinced by the strong case that societies gain more from open and critical debate about marginal, challenging or offensive views than from their exclusion – whether on the grounds that this is essential for establishing truth, for participating in democracy, or because the consequences of exclusion are worse. Whilst it is obviously true that university events are not the only way in which students can listen to such views (an argument often put forward by advocates of no-platforming), we believe that universities *should* be places where such voices are heard and rigorously scrutinised, and that students should be able to organise campus debate about these views if they wish.

The Charity Commission argues that hosting controversial speakers can undermine a students' union's reputation (which would mean the trustees are failing to comply with charity law). Undoubtedly this is a real risk. But as confirmed in the Equality and Human Rights Commission (EHRC)'s guidance for students' unions, it can also be damaging to a union's and its university's reputation if they choose *not* to host controversial speakers (EHRC, 2019: 21). If students' unions are expected only to host speakers that fulfil the Charity Commission's apparently narrow understanding of what is beneficial for the public, then some will be inclined to turn down requests for speakers who represent marginal or unorthodox views. This undermines the unions' reputation and that of their parent universities as places of critical debate.

Beyond this, our case study highlights how the Charity Commission relies strongly on media reports of charity events and uses these to assess whether or not an individual is extreme or controversial. This means that charities are expected to anticipate and mitigate the risk not only that a speaker actually holds or will express extreme views, but also that media outlets will *perceive* the speaker as espousing such views. The Commission alluded to this in its written submission to the JCHR inquiry, noting that when looking at external speakers 'the Commission often will not focus on whether or not the speaker or event *is* in fact controversial or goes beyond the point of being controversial to being considered "extreme" [emphasis added]' but instead will focus on other factors, such as the extent to which trustees have assessed the level of risk that reputational damage may arise from the event (Charity Commission, 2018: 18). If a media outlet claims a charity like a students' union has hosted someone extreme, then in effect the charity has already failed in its legal duty to protect its reputation.

Others share our concerns about excessive (particularly right-wing populist) media influence on the Commission's work since Shawcross's period as Chair. The Directory of Social Change has developed a toolkit for measuring the Commission's independence from government and the media and states that sector commentators should ask whether the Commission 'has reacted according to facts or evidence' or has 'jumped on the bandwagon in reaction to a negative story' in the media, responding 'in a way that gives the impression of satisfying popular "demands" for change' (Directory of Social Change, 2018: 3–4). Our research suggests the Commission needs to do more to reassure the sector of its independence.

Our case study demonstrates how there is no right of appeal against the categorisation of an individual as extreme or controversial; these labels are sticky. Even if it can be demonstrated that an individual does not, or no longer, holds the views considered problematic, if media outlets have labelled her as such, she remains a risk to the charity's reputation. This was demonstrated in our case study. Regarding one of the controversial speakers, the students' union demonstrated to the Charity Commission that the speaker had published in-depth articles renouncing his past offensive comments. Yet a few months after the Commission received this information, it launched investigations into a number of Muslim charities for hosting the same speaker.

There are important implications of all this for freedom of speech on campus. At no point did the Commission's officer state that the controversial speakers should not have been invited. Yet it was quite clear that the Commission disapproved of the union's decision to host them (in some cases without explaining why) and wished to discourage it from inviting similar people in the future. Thus it encouraged the union to adopt a risk-averse no-platforming approach as a default position for such speakers. If the Commission adopts a similar approach when investigating other students' unions, it is highly likely that some will feel pressured to turn down requests from students for speakers who have previously garnered media criticism, thereby limiting the range of debate on campus.

Moreover, the Charity Commission's regulatory approach disproportionately affects the freedom of speech of Muslim speakers and members of Palestine and Islamic Societies, by encouraging unions to be particularly risk-averse when managing these groups' activities.

Finally, the lack of any explicit criteria by which Commission officers determine whether a particular speaker is, or is not, 'controversial' means that Commission interventions into universities can appear arbitrary. For example, in our case study, the Commission focused only on the activities of the Palestine and Islamic Societies, whilst in the period of correspondence, Israel's ambassador to the United Kingdom visited the same university as part of a tour of about 20 universities. The ambassador's visit, which was upon the invitation of student societies and therefore of the students' union, went ahead successfully, but he was met with a large student protest (as was the case at several other universities he visited) outside the building. Yet the Charity Commission did not mention his visit in their correspondence to the students' union, even though the event was discussed in the media, and did not question why he was not partnered by someone else challenging his views (on the Israel/Palestine conflict), as it had insisted in the case of Muslim speakers. This event was a good example of how the freedom of speech of controversial speakers, their supporters and those who disagree with them can all be upheld on campus. We question, however, why the Charity Commission did not consider this high-profile event to be 'controversial' enough to merit comment; this suggests inconsistency in their approach.

Conclusion

The Charity Commission is becoming an important, though often overlooked, agent in the politics of freedom of speech on campus, and the politics of extremism in the charity sector more widely. Although it is generally a light-touch regulator, some students' unions who have been subject to its intervention, particularly those reputed to have highly politically active student bodies, are being encouraged by it to be highly risk-averse. This furthers our findings from Chapter 5: students' unions that have faced scrutiny from the Charity Commission are not only being pushed towards guarded liberalism, but also towards the no-platforming approach as a default position when it comes to speakers who are *perceived* by others, especially in the populist right-wing media, to be controversial.

This position is consistent with Waldron's advocacy of restrictions on hate speech, and with Sorial's argument that universities have a ('negative') duty to exclude and delegitimise extremists (Sorial, 2012: 165; Waldron, 2012). But we align more with Heinze (2016) and consider this a dangerous development that undermines universities' role of being spaces where the dominant orthodoxies of society can be tested and challenged. This is particularly the case because, unlike in Waldron and Sorial's hypothetical reasoning, it appears that in practice it is not just people with undeniably racist or hateful views but others with more ambiguous views who are being affected by this push to risk aversion.

While the Charity Commission has no obligation to uphold freedom of speech, it is remarkable to witness it downplay student entitlement to some form of Kantian categorical imperative (to treat others fairly in the hope of being treated fairly oneself), and the freedom to host the speakers they want, not only to listen to them but to debate them and make up their own minds.

Our research also shows that on campus, the concepts of 'extreme' and 'controversial' are shaped not by objective criteria but primarily by the subjective assumptions of officials working for the Charity Commission and by media allegations. Because Muslim speakers face more media scrutiny than others in this sector, this means that Charity Commission interventions on campus are particularly likely to involve Muslims. If this approach continues, the overall effect could be that students' unions with higher ethnic minority representation, fewer resources, weaker university backing or less determination to take risks may well choose not to host specifically Muslim speakers deemed to have 'controversial' views. In such a scenario, Muslim students would rightly feel that they are less able to hold debates on difficult political and social issues than other students.

Finally, all this shows how one of the narratives of moral panic about universities (that they are allowing extremists to operate with impunity) affects universities through their external regulators; the Charity Commission encourages risk aversion *as if* students are abusing their right to freedom of speech. It appears to have no interest in actually facilitating productive debate about complex topics. Positive reinforcement of students' interest in developing their responsibilities as citizens would be more productive. In the final chapter, we suggest how universities can do this, resisting risk aversion by pursuing a culture of reciprocity and deliberative democracy.

Notes

1 CAGE describes itself as lobbying against 'repressive state policies' initiated under the War on Terror (CAGE, n.d.).
2 For a discussion of the project, see Chapter 4.
3 See Chapter 5 for an explanation of charitable objects and the public benefit.

References

Cabinet Office, Prime Minister's Office and Rt Hon David Cameron (2014) 'New Funding and Powers to Tackle Abuse in the Charity Sector'. Press Release, 22 October. https://www.gov.uk/government/news/new-funding-and-powers-to-tackle-abuse-in-the-charity-sector.
CAGE (n.d.) 'About Us'. https://www.cage.ngo/about-us.
Charity Commission (2018) 'Further Written Evidence from the Charity Commission for England and Wales'. In Joint Committee on Human Rights (2018) *Freedom of Speech in Universities*. Written evidence, FSU0109. https://publications.parliament.uk/pa/jt201719/jtselect/jtrights/589/589.pdf.
Charity Commission (2019) *Charity Commission Operational Guidance*. OG 48, 'Students' Unions'. http://ogs.charitycommission.gov.uk/g048a001.aspx.

Civil Exchange (2015) *An Independent Mission: The Voluntary Sector in 2015*. Civil Exchange. http://www.civilexchange.org.uk/wp-content/uploads/2015/02/Independence-Panel-Report_An-Independent-Mission-PR.pdf.

Cook, S. (2015) 'The Charity Commission, Cage, the High Court and the Revealing Emails', *Third Sector*, 19 November. http://www.thirdsector.co.uk/charity-commission-cage-high-court-revealing-emails/governance/article/1373100.

Cooney, R. (2016) 'Charity Commission Has Cut Workforce by 10 Per Cent, Annual Report Shows', *ThirdSector*, 7 July. https://www.thirdsector.co.uk/charity-commission-cut-workforce-10-per-cent-annual-report-shows/governance/article/1401619.

Delmar-Morgan, A. (2015) 'Islamic Charities in UK Fear They Are Being Unfairly Targeted over Extremism', *The Guardian*, 22 July. https://www.theguardian.com/society/2015/jul/22/muslim-charities-uk-targeted-extremism-fears.

Directory of Social Change (2018) *The Three Pillars of Independence*. London: Directory of Social Change. https://www.dsc.org.uk/wp-content/uploads/2018/05/here.pdf.

Equality and Human Rights Commission (2019) *Freedom of Expression in England and Wales: A Guide for Higher Education Providers and Students' Unions in England and Wales*. https://www.equalityhumanrights.com/sites/default/files/freedom-of-expression-guide-for-higher-education-providers-and-students-unions-england-and-wales.pdf.

Gamsu, S. and Donnelly, M. (2017) *Diverse Places of Learning? Home Neighbourhood Ethnic Diversity and the Ethnic Composition of Universities*. Institute for Policy Research Policy Belief. Bath: University of Bath. https://www.bath.ac.uk/publications/diverse-places-of-learning-home-neighbourhood-ethnic-diversity-ethnic-composition-of-universities/.

Heinze, E. (2016) *Hate Speech and Democratic Citizenship*. Oxford: Oxford University Press.

Holmes, T. (2014) 'The Charity Commission's Board: An Impartial Watchdog?' *Spinwatch*, 12 March. http://spinwatch.org/index.php/issues/politics/item/5627-charity-commission-article.

Home Office (2011) *Prevent Strategy*. House of Commons Cm 8092. London: The Stationery Office. https://www.gov.uk/government/publications/prevent-strategy-2011.

Home Office (2019) *Prevent Duty Guidance: For Higher Education Institutions in England and Wales*. https://www.gov.uk/government/publications/prevent-duty-guidance/prevent-duty-guidance-for-higher-education-institutions-in-england-and-wales.

Ironmonger, J. (2017) 'Concerns Raised over Students' Unions' Anti-Israel Stance', *BBC News*, 27 April. https://www.bbc.co.uk/news/uk-39719314.

Kant, I. (2002) *Groundwork for the Metaphysics of Morals*. Edited and translated by A.W. Wood. Binghamton, NY: Vail-Ballou Press. First published in 1785.

Kay, L. (2017) 'Regulator Contacts Students' Unions over Israel Boycott Stance', *Third Sector*, 28 April. https://www.thirdsector.co.uk/regulator-contacts-students-unions-israel-boycott-stance/governance/article/1431921.

Kennedy, J. and Ferrell-Schweppenstedde, D. (2018) 'New Toolkit Revealed to Question Charity Regulator's Political Independence', *Directory of Social Change*, 15 May. https://www.dsc.org.uk/content/new-toolkit-revealed-to-question-charity-regulators-political-independence/.

Mason, T. (2014) 'Commission Unfairly Targets Muslim Charities, Says Think Tank', *Civil Society News*, 17 November. https://www.civilsociety.co.uk/news/commission-unfairly-targets-muslim-charities--says-think-tank.html.

Mukadam, M. and Scott-Baumann, A. with Chowdhary, A. and Contractor, S. (2010) *The Training and Development of Muslim Faith Leaders: Current Practice and Future Possibilities*. London: Department for Communities and Local Government. https://assets.publishing.service.gov.uk/government/uploads/system/uploads/attachment_data/file/6155/1734121.pdf.

National Audit Office (2013) *The Regulatory Effectiveness of the Charity Commission*. London: The Stationery Office. https://www.nao.org.uk/report/regulatory-effectiveness-charity-commission-2/.

Pudelek, J. (2014) 'Bubb: Charity Commission Is "Targeting Muslim Charities" in a Disproportionate Way', *Civil Society News*, 3 July. https://www.civilsociety.co.uk/news/bubb--charity-commission-is--targeting-muslim-charities-in-a-disproportionate-way-.html.

Ramesh, R. (2014) 'Quarter of Charity Commission Inquiries Target Muslim Groups', *The Guardian*, 16 November. https://www.theguardian.com/society/2014/nov/16/charity-commission-inquiries-muslim-groups.

Ramesh, R. (2015) 'Charities Can Fund Cage Campaign Group, Commission Agrees', *The Guardian*, 21 October. https://www.theguardian.com/society/2015/oct/21/charities-can-fund-controversial-pressure-group-cage-court-finds.

Scott-Baumann, A. and Tomlinson, H. (2016) 'Cultural Cold Wars: The Risk of Anti-"extremism" Policy for Academic Freedom of Expression'. SOAS, 15 June. https://blogs.soas.ac.uk/muslimwise/2016/06/15/question-time-cultural-cold-wars-the-risk-of-anti-extremism-policy-for-academic-freedom-of-expression-alison-scott-baumann-and-hugh-tomlinson-qc/.

Slater, A. (2018) 'Challenging the Legitimacy of Extremism'. In Panjwani, F., Revell, L., Gholami, R., and Diboll, M. (eds.) *Education and Extremisms: Rethinking Liberal Pedagogies in the Contemporary World*. Abingdon: Routledge: 91–104.

Sorial, S. (2012) *Sedition and the Advocacy of Violence: Free Speech and Counter-Terrorism*. London: Routledge.

Strauss, D.A. (1991) 'Persuasion, Autonomy, and Freedom of Expression', *Columbia Law Review*, 91: 334–371. https://core.ac.uk/download/pdf/207571931.pdf.

ThirdSector (2013) Analysis: 'An Emphasis on Regulation and a Move Toward the Right', 13 May. https://www.thirdsector.co.uk/analysis-an-emphasis-regulation-move-toward-right/governance/article/1182014.

Turner, C. (2014) 'Government Donation to Muslim Charities Forum Denounced as "Madness"', *The Telegraph*, 23 September https://www.telegraph.co.uk/news/uknews/11114599/Government-donation-to-Muslim-Charities-Forum-denounced-as-madness.html.

Waldron, J. (2012) *The Harm in Hate Speech*. Cambridge, MA: Harvard University Press.

7 Improving conversations about difficult topics

The term *free speech* implies that we are free to speak: but free to say what exactly?

For some universities, speaking freely now means speaking in ways that will satisfy the government. At the time of writing in the summer 2020, Gavin Williamson, the Secretary of State for Education, stated that emergency funding for universities in the COVID-19 crisis would be conditional upon, amongst other issues, an institution's commitment to freedom of speech. Students' unions would be required to focus on 'serving the needs of the wider student population rather than subsidising niche activism and campaigns', which again suggests those outside universities will decide what is good free speech and what is bad free speech (Adams, 2020). He has also instructed universities to adopt the controversial International Holocaust Remembrance Alliance's (IHRA) definition of anti-Semitism (Busby, 2020)[1]. These are unprecedented interventions.

But it is also the logical outcome for a sector with a distorted public image. Students are routinely mocked and feared in public debate, being presented as illiberal 'snowflakes' who weaken freedom of speech and melt at the slightest hint of controversy, or (if they are Muslim) as proto-terrorists who encourage extreme speakers and foster radicalisation. You cannot be both snowflake *and* firebrand. These narratives of moral panic are driven by external groups that push staff and students towards the extreme approaches to freedom of speech: towards libertarianism (seeing the exercise of one's right to freedom of speech as paramount above others' rights), or towards no-platforming (the ultimate end of a tendency to view the exercise of speech as a risk to be managed). Right-wing populist leaders sneak into the gap between these narratives, pointing to both to fuel their claim that key institutions of liberal democracy are failing the 'people', and that authoritarian solutions are needed to wrest back control from the 'liberal elite'.

In this book we have shown that these narratives are false. Radicalisation into terrorism is extremely rare in UK universities, and the number of formal referrals made to Channel/Prevent Professional Concerns by universities is tiny. Freedom of speech on campus is not facing a major crisis, and the vast majority of speaker events requested on campus are upheld (Office for Students [OfS], 2019: 10). Students themselves have diverse, and increasingly polarised, views about freedom of speech, but overwhelmingly they value it as an important principle, and most say they feel free to express their views.

Yet sometimes, the concern of some students to protect the rights of vulnerable groups can mean they refuse to engage with opposing views. There is evidence that a minority of students do not feel as free to speak as they would wish to in the classroom – including students with rightwing or socially conservative views. While the scale of this effect is not as great as implied in popular discourse, nonetheless university staff should take it seriously. As we argue later, they should work consciously to create a culture of open debate in the classroom, by developing a Community of Inquiry (CofI). This is necessary to overcome the inhibiting polarisation on campus, which is being exacerbated by the political and media narratives about students and wider global events.

In this book we have focused particularly on regulatory structures that can chill freedom of speech on campus – particularly for Muslim students. The weight of evidence from the major *Re/presenting Islam on Campus* project (Guest et al., 2020) confirms that the operation of the Prevent Duty on campus has made many Muslim students feel uncomfortable and worried about being unfairly scrutinised, breaking down trust between students and lecturers, even when they have not personally encountered Prevent. Some are censoring their speech on controversial topics and are avoiding risk in their classroom contributions, research choices and external speaker requests (Scott-Baumann et al., 2020). More widely, Muslim women in particular worry about experiencing Islamophobia on campus, and the university space, as with other public spaces, remains a male-gendered one. Mary Beard believes suppression of the female voice is as bad today as it was in ancient Greece, where 'public speech was a – if not the – defining attribute of maleness' (Beard, 2017: 17).

We have also addressed a new issue in this debate, showing that the regulatory approach of the Charity Commission for England and Wales encourages some students' union chief executives and other staff to be risk-averse, and there is a danger that this can lead to students' unions turning down students' requests for controversial, lawful speakers. This is a problem because the inviting students are denied an opportunity to take ownership of their learning experience and to generate debate on campus. It also undermines students' ability to interrogate a wide range of views; learning about ideas from an article or video, for example, does not give them the same educational opportunity as a speaker event where they can engage with and challenge a speaker and debate with others.

These two structures have been pushing universities and students' unions towards guarded liberalism and pre-emptive no-platforming as a default position when handling requests for speakers with controversial views; in turn, this pushes students and sabbatical officers to be risk-averse when organising events. This weakens the ability of universities to fulfil one of their key purposes – to make space in society for rigorous debate about difficult issues.

How should universities respond to all this? In the rest of this chapter we show how universities can reform their structures and pedagogies and support student debate both on campus and beyond. Part of this involves encouraging the development of deliberative democracy: where ordinary citizens come together to debate issues that affect them and are empowered to make practical change (Chwalisz, 2019). Universities should foster such spaces on campus, giving students a greater say in the structures that affect them. Developing deliberative democracy means creating and protecting opportunities for open debate to develop group decision making so that young people have a voice. It also means building stronger links between universities and the corridors of power at Parliament, so that academics and students' research and voices can influence policymaking directly.

Reforming university structures

Universities need to respond actively and positively to the problematic impact of the two regulatory structures.

University managers should accept that a significant proportion of Muslim students and others feel alienated by the Prevent Duty. They should ensure that students and academics have appropriate representation on Prevent working groups and should hold direct, open conversations with Muslim students and Islamic Societies to hear their concerns and discuss how to alleviate them. Such dialogue cannot be a one-off but must become a regular feature of campus life to ensure that each new cohort of students feels heard. This will address the democratic deficit in universities, where students are subjected to inhibiting structures over which they have no influence.

University managers should also recognise that the Prevent Duty does not require them to prevent external people with controversial views from speaking. As clarified in the Salman Butt case, universities must consider the government's Prevent Duty Guidance, but are not obliged to follow it to any particular outcome. They can choose to prioritise their duty to uphold freedom of speech, including for people with extreme (but lawful) views (*R (on the application of Salman Butt) v The Secretary of the State for the Home Department*. [2019]).

More fundamentally, our evidence calls into question the need for the Prevent Duty. Radicalisation is not really a problem in universities, and some of our Prevent Lead interviewees doubted that the time and money spent on setting up Prevent training and associated structures has made a significant difference to the protection of students. Currently, universities are legally required to comply with the Duty and will face sanctions if they do not. But they should push back against the securitisation of the sector and the public tendency to treat Muslims as objects of suspicion. It is imperative that universities and students' unions engage in the upcoming review of Prevent to try to influence the future of the strategy (Home Office, 2019).

In terms of charity law, the Charity Commission updated its guidance for English and Welsh students' unions in 2018, conceding that they can host controversial debates, and that freedom of speech should form part of their 'fundamental consideration' when pursuing their charitable objects (Charity Commission, 2019: OG 48, Section 7.1). This is an important step in the right direction, partly driven by our submission of evidence reprised in this book to the inquiry of the Joint Committee on Human Rights (JCHR) in 2017–18. The Charity Commission should be mindful of this and ensure that in its regulation of students' unions, it does not pressure them to avoid controversial debates or speakers.

Students' unions, meanwhile, should be allowed to choose to uphold freedom of speech, including for speakers with controversial views. Students' union trustees have a charitable duty to protect their union's reputation, but there is reputational risk in cancelling events as well as in allowing them to proceed (Equality and Human Rights Commission, 2019: 20–21). We want students' unions to be more concerned about creating space for rigorous, open debate on campus, and less concerned about trying to avoid negative media coverage. If they are worried about the reputational risk of hosting a particular speaker, the students' union could also consider asking their parent university to host the speaker, as universities are less constrained by the Charity Commission.

At the time of writing, as Black Lives Matter protests sweep the globe and we face an unprecedented economic crisis following COVID-19, we envisage live issues that students will rightly want to use their unions' resources for, but which do not fit the requirement that they only fund activities that further their educational interests (Charity Commission, 2019). These include funding campaigns against police brutality or against government responses to the pandemic that exacerbate economic inequality for students and others. If students vote to fund such campaigns, their union trustees should find a way to justify the activism as broadly serving their educational charitable objects. Our political life will be greatly diminished if students' unions are depoliticised.

Political intervention into campus life is currently unprecedentedly high and it is therefore necessary to make sure that students are fully consulted about Prevent and fully informed about the Charity Commission. Ideology is used to legitimise power, which can be uplifting and emancipatory, or restrictive. We need free exploration of the ideologies that shape our politics, and idealistic, utopian imagination about how life could be different. This requires hopefulness, optimism and clear, explicit organisation of group discussion, in line with Hankinson Nelson's (1993) advocacy of a community-centred approach for developing new ideas.

Reforming university pedagogy: deliberative democracy

Lasting change in how universities handle freedom of speech can only occur when universities themselves take the lead, by providing students with explicit guidance for engaging in difficult debate and including them in dialogue with staff about what freedom of speech should look like in different contexts on campus. Such teaching needs to be available to all students – including in disciplines outside the Humanities, where students may have less opportunity currently to engage in debate.

Instead of the simplistic binary of more or less freedom of speech, students and staff need a fresh understanding of the options available when considering how to handle a discussion or event on a divisive topic. Our fourfold model of freedom of speech provides this and enables people to make *active* decisions about which approach is appropriate for each situation. This can be used as part of the development of a CofI, which is essential for reforming pedagogy on campus. It can help to ensure that all have a voice and can also address sexism by changing the structure of discussion so that each participant (of whatever gender) can speak. As Beard explains: 'You cannot easily fit women into a structure that is coded as male: you have to change the structure' (Beard, 2017: 86–87).

The CofI pedagogy was first developed by the pragmatist philosopher C.S. Peirce. It is a practical mechanism for managing group discussion on complex or divisive issues and creates the conversational tools for developing deliberative democracy. Deliberative democracy resembles Mouffe's agonistic approach, and in 2019 Chwalisz (2019) celebrated 'a new wave of contemporary deliberative democracy, based on the premise that political decisions should be the result of reasonable discussion among citizens'. Deliberative bodies such as citizens' councils, assemblies, and juries are often called 'deliberative mini-publics' in academic literature. They are just one aspect of deliberative democracy and involve randomly selected citizens spending a significant period of time developing informed recommendations for public authorities. In the CofI pedagogy, participants may come together over multiple sessions, building relationships of trust and a sense of collaboration in learning. They are encouraged to ask each other questions, probing each other's and their own ideas and hidden assumptions regarding an issue. A trained facilitator (a lecturer or a student) manages the process, but the ground rules for the discussion are established at the start by the participants themselves, giving them ownership of the conversation. Most importantly, the participants agree in advance to follow a set of *procedural values*, such as showing respect for others, tolerance of different viewpoints, and active listening. In typical seminar discussions such values tend to be assumed but are rarely discussed explicitly. The active discussion of these underlying procedural values, and of the parameters for the conversation, makes CofI different, bringing the fine tradition of consent training, mediation and conflict resolution that is already present on campus directly into class debate and student meetings (Pardales and Girod, 2006; Scott-Baumann, 2010).

We build on previous theoretical work about CofI by adding our fourfold model of freedom of speech as a key element. We suggest that participants need to agree in advance to the approach to freedom of speech that will govern their discussion or event. Such active work can help participants to share risk, becoming risk-aware rather than risk-averse – exercising their right to freedom of speech confidently, whilst also thinking responsibly about how that might affect others. In the Appendix, we show how this can be done practically and the procedures underpinning it.

As a default position, we encourage students and staff to pursue the liberal approach to freedom of speech. This means upholding freedom of speech as far as possible within the law, including for offensive views, up to the point where it is clearly likely to harm others or infringe their rights. But it also means encouraging people to avoid language (but not topics or ideas) that many others are likely to find grossly offensive or hateful (distinguishing it from libertarianism). The liberal approach allows universities to be places where difficult ideas – including marginal and unorthodox ones – can be debated and challenged openly. We support Butler (1997, 2015), Heinze (2016) and Strauss (1991) in their view that controversial, divisive topics should be discussed as far as possible.

Part of speaking freely in a multifaith campus also means allowing students, if they so wish, to make arguments using religious reasoning. As Habermas argues, religious reasoning should not be silenced, if only for the reason that doing so may cut society off 'from key resources for the creation of meaning and identity' (Habermas, 2006: 10). Students thus can feel they bring their whole selves to the learning environment and are not faced with an asymmetric burden that non-religious students do not face. Classroom tutors should be aware of the implicit assumption that only secular-based reasoning is neutral and 'acceptable' and try to make certain space for religious reasoning.

Making space for religious reasoning entails accepting possible criticism of those arguments, however. The CofI demands that we accept the person even though we may reject their ideas. The liberal approach in particular demands such critique because underpinning it is the (ultimately secular) assumption that people share, broadly speaking, similar underlying beliefs and values, including a belief that everything should be open to criticism. This view is widely shared in universities. It is, however, an unavoidable limitation to the liberal approach because in particular debates, for example about deeply held religious beliefs, it can privilege some people over others, such as students who do not hold strong religious beliefs over those who do. Using the CofI approach reminds us to find a human bond with others even when we think their ideas are stupid.

In some cases, students and staff may decide reasonably that some topics or ideas are so complex, delicate or offensive that they need to deviate from the default liberal approach and choose guarded liberalism instead. This approach assumes some self-censorship and careful choice of vocabulary, which may need to be agreed upon in advance. Different guarded liberal measures restrict freedom of speech to different extents. Requiring an external speaker to submit a speech in advance for vetting will limit freedom of speech more than requiring an event to have a balanced panel or discouraging the use of certain terms in a classroom discussion. These measures do, however, make it possible for debate to go ahead, by making it more likely that vulnerable groups will feel comfortable joining, and (in some cases) by focusing on consensus-building rather than confrontational disagreement between opposing binary views.

Guarded liberalism is much to be preferred to the no-platforming approach. However, occasionally a no-platforming approach may actually help to facilitate discussion. For example, participants may agree in advance not to discuss a particularly divisive aspect of an issue, allowing them to continue discussing the topic in more general terms.

Occasionally, participants in a discussion or event may agree to adopt the libertarian approach, with no restrictions at all on any divisive topic or language (as long as it remains within the law). This can be useful for allowing classes to explore a divisive issue to its fullest extent, for example, but it carries the most risk of creating deep offence.

All four approaches to freedom of speech have merits and drawbacks. Each can be used flexibly, including in combination within the same event, to enable the careful exploration of difficult issues. This requires participants to have active discussions about what kind of approach(es) they wish to take on a case-by-case basis and to agree in advance what the parameters of their discussions should be. Sometimes it will be difficult to reach agreement about this – in which case, the guarded liberal approach should be adopted, which at least allows debate to go ahead.

The CofI approach can help encourage a culture of reciprocity, wherein participants in a discussion recognise that they have obligations to each other, including to people they disagree with. In particular, they should see themselves obliged to allow each other a right to reply; to avoid misrepresenting each other; to listen to each other; and to hold open a space to allow each other to learn. There can be reciprocity even in adversity; when arguing against each other's views, participants are encouraged to see each other as collaborators in the learning process and to assume that everyone has well-intentioned rather than bad faith motives. This aligns with Ricoeur's (2006) view of speech as a moral action entailing responsibilities on participants. It is a necessary corrective to the simplistic 'us v them' narratives that underpin populist discourse and that reduce one's political opponents to a homogenous enemy.

Building this culture of reciprocity takes time and depends on participants trusting each other. Thus it is most likely to arise through ongoing, facilitated classroom discussions. But student societies also have a critical role in nurturing reciprocity on campus, by using CofI principles to manage their internal discussions and public events. Students' union staff should build learning about these principles, and about the fourfold model of freedom of speech, into their annual training for student societies.

Universities need to provide stronger support to these societies – especially to faith and belief societies like Islamic Societies, which, along with Palestine Societies, face more external scrutiny of their events programmes than other student groups. Research from the think tank, Theos, has shown the essential contribution these societies can make to student life, by providing pastoral and spiritual support and building bridges between different groups. Yet many of them face organisational and logistical challenges that limit their potential. By doing more to listen to these societies and providing students' union staff time to help them reach their goals, universities can build greater trust with students (Perfect et al., 2019).

CofI principles can also be useful for external speaker events. At the start of such events, organisers should encourage the audiences to see themselves as active participants in the educational process and as helping to build a space where all can develop their critical analysis skills. Where an event or speaker is flagged as potentially controversial, the university or students' union management should have open conversations with the organising students or staff (and perhaps with the speaker(s) as well). Starting from the premise that the event should go ahead if possible, they should discuss which approach to freedom of speech is most appropriate, to get the best balance between upholding freedom of speech and protecting students from grievous offence. Using the fourfold model transparently can also be a way for the management to explain to students, and to the speakers, why a particular decision has been made.

Finally, universities should recognise the importance of theology as a resource for handling issues to do with freedom of speech and extremism. As we saw in Chapter 1, important arguments for freedom of speech can be made from religious reasoning – including Islamic reasoning. Failure to engage with such ideas means that freedom of speech is generally seen as a secular value – including by religious extremists who seek to limit the freedom of others to speak. By explicitly acknowledging the religious, as well as secular, arguments for wide freedom of speech, universities can at once resist these extreme narratives and bolster appreciation of that freedom among their diverse student population.

Changing the public narrative through a proactive media strategy

As well as reforming internal structures and pedagogy, university managers need to do more to counter the binary narrative of moral panic being forced on them by external groups, populist leaders and sensationalist media. UK universities tend to be reactive, responding defensively to critical media stories when they arise, rather than proactively publicising their creation of spaces for debate about important, divisive issues.

We showed in Chapter 4 how flawed are the analyses of Higher Education offered by external groups like the Henry Jackson Society and *Spiked*. Rather than ignoring these groups, or responding only when they publish a new report, universities should take the initiative in breaking down and rebuffing their analysis publicly, in a coordinated way. The sector should also be proactive in publicising a more realistic picture of what is going on in universities – especially with so little radicalisation on campus.

Individual universities also need to be better at explaining, transparently, how they are handling freedom of speech. We encourage them to build the fourfold model of freedom of speech into their Freedom of Speech codes and to explain this publicly. For example, universities could state on their websites that they adopt the liberal approach to freedom of speech as a default position, but occasionally another approach may be appropriate, after dialogue with relevant parties. They could also state the number of events requested each year by students (and, separately, by staff), and how many went ahead. If any requests were turned down, explanations could be given in a way that preserves the anonymity of the organisers and speakers. Universities and students' unions must also maintain records for why particular decisions were made about requested external speakers, in case they need to justify them subsequently.

When hosting a high-profile, controversial speaker, universities should expect a media backlash. This should not be a reason for turning down the event unless the reputational damage is likely to be grievous and long-lasting. When responding to media criticism, universities should position themselves as providing spaces for debate, which is one of their essential, legally protected contributions to liberal democracy. Consequently, they may need to make decisions regarding controversial speakers that other institutions would not. They can point to their strong legal duty to uphold freedom of speech and also to the fourfold model to explain why they made their particular decisions. Releasing recordings of such debates, if appropriate, could also show that public concerns are unjustified.

Connecting students and academics to people with power

In Chapter 2 we argued that in order to hold governments to account and to combat rising hate speech, we need to retain the energy of populism and its desire to speak truth to power. There are various ways university staff can build stronger pathways to Parliament. Here are two approaches drawn from our own experiences:

- Engaging with Select Committees and APPGs

Select Committees, such as the Joint Committee on Human Rights (JCHR), play important roles in holding public inquiries and holding government to account. All-Party Parliamentary Groups (APPGs) are informal cross-party groups with less power, but which can still instigate inquiries and drive national debate – as the APPG on British Muslims did with an enquiry on defining Islamophobia in 2018 (APPGBM, 2018). Some APPGs organise regular panel events that are open to the public, which can give students a point of access to parliamentary life.

Universities need to do more to encourage and support academics and students in submitting evidence to such inquiries. An example of this kind of engagement is our own participation in the JCHR's 2017 inquiry into freedom of speech on campus. Through previous work, Perfect had connections with one of the Committee's MPs. When the MP asked her contacts for initial advice on the issues, Perfect provided a briefing paper about the impact of the Charity Commission for England and Wales on students' unions' freedom of speech; this shaped the direction of the enquiry, by prompting the JCHR to analyse the role of the Charity Commission.

Scott-Baumann was cited as an expert by Paul Bowen, a QC working on the *Butt* case and thus was invited to give oral evidence to the JCHR about our research (JCHR, 2018). By working with the clerk to the JCHR, she secured invitations for two students (Dr Alyaa Ebbiary and Lottie Moore) to provide oral evidence. They were the only student voices on the panel and provided material evidence that significantly advanced the inquiry. The evidence we and the students provided led the JCHR to make important recommendations for the Charity Commission in their final report.

- Building a bank of briefing papers for policymakers, and training students to engage with them

Universities should also be proactive in helping academics and students to influence parliamentarians and civil servants outside the context of specific inquiries. They could establish a team (including students, where possible) to help academics summarise their research into short briefing papers for policymakers. The team could also provide training opportunities for students and staff to learn how to lobby parliamentarians effectively.

An example of this is Influencing Corridors of Power (ICOP), an initiative established at SOAS in 2020 by Scott-Baumann and a team of academics and students (Dr Rob Faure Walker, Dr Maryyum Mehmood, Dr Alyaa Ebbiary, Shahanaz Begum, Rana Osman, Lottie Moore and Hasan Pandor) https://blogs.soas.ac.uk/cop/. The team helps expert academics and students produce high-quality briefing papers on matters of urgent interest, which are published on a website and emailed to all MPs and all members of the House of Lords. The team holds discussions with policymakers, conducts media interviews and instigates the submission of formal questions (via MPs) to government ministers. They have also produced guidance documents for students explaining how, for example, bills pass through Parliament (Faure Walker, 2020).

Conclusion

As universities prepare to face an unprecedented economic crisis, they can no longer afford to ignore the false narratives that are eating away at their reputations. They must rearticulate to a disillusioned public why they are so critical to liberal democracy and work to develop deliberative democracy though the Community of Inquiry and lobbying. Negotiated freedom of speech is central to this.

Universities and students' unions must find new ways to create spaces where controversial topics can be debated and where challenging, even offensive, voices can be heard and subjected to rigorous scrutiny. But they can only do so if they resist the pressures pushing them and their students towards risk aversion. In particular, they must take seriously the concerns of Muslim students about structures that are pushing some of them to self-censorship.

Most importantly, they must take concrete steps to teach students how to talk with, and listen to, people they disagree with strongly. Education in participating in dialogue is largely absent in our society, leaving us unable to resist the relentless polarisation driven by our political culture and social media addiction. But it does not have to be this way. We can learn to discuss better, and we can learn to listen well through deliberative democratic processes. Universities must put such learning at the heart of their offering to society.

Note

1. For a discussion of the pros and cons of the IHRA definition, see Sedley et al. (2018).

References

Legal cases

R (on the application of Salman Butt) v The Secretary of the State for the Home Department. [2019] EWCA Civ 256. https://www.judiciary.uk/wp-content/uploads/2019/03/r-butt-v-sshd-judgment.pdf.

Secondary sources

Adams, R. (2020) 'English Universities Must Prove "Commitment" to Free Speech for Bailouts', *The Guardian*, 16 July. https://www.theguardian.com/education/2020/jul/16/english-universities-must-prove-commitment-to-free-speech-for-bailouts.

All Party Parliamentary Group on British Muslims (2018) *Islamophobia Defined*. London: All Party Parliamentary Group on British Muslims. https://static1.squarespace.com/static/599c3d2febbd1a90cffdd8a9/t/5bfd1ea3352f531a6170ceee/1543315109493/Islamophobia+Defined.pdf.

Beard, M. (2017) *Women & Power: A Manifesto*. London: Profile Books Ltd.

Busby, E. (2020) 'Universities May Face Cuts If They Reject Definition of Antisemitism, Says Education Minister', *The Independent*, 9 October. https://www.independent.co.uk/news/education/education-news/antisemitism-universities-gavin-williamson-funding-cuts-b911500.html

Butler, J. (1997) *Excitable Speech: A Politics of the Performative*. New York: Routledge.

Butler, J. (2015) *Notes Towards a Performative Theory of Assembly*. Cambridge, MA: Harvard University Press.

Charity Commission (2019) *Charity Commission Operational Guidance*. OG 48, 'Students' Unions'. http://ogs.charitycommission.gov.uk/g048a001.aspx.

Chwalisz, C. (2019) 'A New Wave of Deliberative Democracy', *Carnegie Europe*, 26 November. https://carnegieeurope.eu/2019/11/26/new-wave-of-deliberative-democracy-pub-80422.

Equality and Human Rights Commission (2019) *Freedom of Expression in England and Wales; A Guide for Higher Education Providers and Students' Unions in England and Wales*. https://www.equalityhumanrights.com/sites/default/files/freedom-of-expression-guide-for-higher-education-providers-and-students-unions-england-and-wales.pdf.

Faure Walker, R. (2020) *Guide to Bills and Acts of Parliament*. SOAS Corridors of Power (COP) Policy Briefings, 1 June. https://blogs.soas.ac.uk/cop/wp-content/uploads/2020/06/How-to-Lobby-for-Changes-to-Bills-and-Acts-of-Parliament.pdf.

Guest, M., Scott-Baumann, A., Cheruvallil-Contractor, S., Naguib, S., Phoenix, A., Lee, Y. and Al Baghal, T. (2020) *Islam and Muslims on UK University Campuses: Perceptions and Challenges*. Durham: Durham University, London: SOAS, Coventry: Coventry University and Lancaster: Lancaster University. https://www.soas.ac.uk/representingislamoncampus/publications/file148310.pdf.

Habermas, J. (2006) 'Religion in the Public Sphere', *European Journal of Philosophy*, 14, 1: 1–25.

Hankinson Nelson, L. (1993) 'Epistemological Communities'. In Alcoff, L. and Potter, E. (eds.) *Feminist Epistemologies*. New York: Routledge: 121–159.

Heinze, E. (2016) *Hate Speech and Democratic Citizenship*. Oxford: Oxford University Press.

Home Office (2019) *Independent Review of Prevent*. London: Home Office. https://www.gov.uk/government/collections/independent-review-of-prevent.

Joint Committee on Human Rights (2018) *Freedom of Speech in Universities*. House of Lords/House of Commons (HC 589). Oral evidence, 17 January. London: The Stationery Office. http://data.parliament.uk/writtenevidence/committeeevidence.svc/evidencedocument/human-rights-committee/freedom-of-speech-in-universities/oral/77341.html.

Office for Students (OfS) (2019) *Prevent Monitoring Accountability and Data Returns 2017–18: Evaluation Report*. London: Office for Students. https://www.officeforstudents.org.uk/media/860e26e2-63e7-47eb-84e0-49100788009c/ofs2019_22.pdf.

Pardales, M.J. and Girod, M. (2006) 'Community of Inquiry: Its Past and Present Future', *Educational Philosophy and Theory*, 38, 3: 299–309.

Perfect, S., Aune, K. and Ryan, B. (2019) *Faith and Belief on Campus: Division and Cohesion. Exploring Student Faith and Belief Societies*. London: Theos. https://www.theosthinktank.co.uk/cmsfiles/Reportfiles/Theos---Faith-and-Belief-on-Campus---Division-and-Cohesion.pdf.

Ricoeur, P. (2006) *On Translation*. Translated by E. Brennan. London: Routledge.

Scott-Baumann, A. (2010) 'A Community of Inquiry: Talking to Muslims'. In Farrar, M. (ed.) *The Study of Islam within Social Science Curricula in UK Universities: Case Studies 1*. Centre for Sociology, Anthropology and Politics, Higher Education Academy: 81–84. https://www.heacademy.ac.uk/system/files/max_farrar_case_studies.pdf.

Scott-Baumann, A., Guest, M., Naguib, S., Cheruvallil-Contractor, S., Phoenix, A., Al Baghal, T. and Lee, Y. (2020) *Islam on Campus: Contested Identities and the Cultures of Higher Education in Britain*. Oxford: Oxford University Press.

Sedley, S., Janner-Klausner, L., Bindman, G., Rose, J. and Kahn-Harris, K. (2018) 'How Should Antisemitism Be Defined?', *The Guardian*, 27 July. https://www.theguardian.com/commentisfree/2018/jul/27/antisemitism-ihra-definition-jewish-writers

Strauss, D.A. (1991) 'Persuasion, autonomy, and freedom of expression', *Columbia Law Review*, 91: 334–371. https://core.ac.uk/download/pdf/207571931.pdf.

Appendix
Community of Inquiry (CofI)

A Community of Inquiry (CofI), first developed by C.S. Peirce, requires a conscious and systematic approach, with every move made explicit between students and staff. Making explicit the implicit assumptions behind conversations also helps to uncover structural and personal biases whilst defusing the conflict for which student participants come prepared. This approach can be adapted for academic debate in class, or students' union discussions about their freedom of speech policies, or a student society interested in working with another student society (e.g., if a Jewish Society and a Palestinian Society wanted to combine (Reiff, 2019)). This will often cause exasperation and necessitate compromise, but it can lead to deal-making that promotes mutual understanding and recognition. The CofI can give experience in deliberative democracy (Chwalisz, 2019).

In the feminist tradition, Hankinson Nelson (1993) and others argue that to construct these new ways of problem-solving and acquire knowledge that is useful, we must move away from dependence upon individualistic models that seek inspiration from a single teacher and develop communal meaning-making that facilitates different viewpoints and accepts a range of beliefs and an appreciation of inclusivity. This is compatible with online learning as well, as seen in Salmon's (2013) 'e-tivities' (online assignments) that emphasise self-reflection and peer support and Lee and Rofe's (2016) requirements for intellectual reflection and a code of conduct agreed by all.

Process of a Community of Inquiry

A CofI can be used to help people talk freely about difficult topics. Participants begin by establishing for themselves a set of ground rules. Sometimes agreeing on these can take time and must be done before the main discussion (training guidelines are available at https://blogs.soas.ac.uk/cop):

Before the discussion:

- Use the fourfold model (liberal, libertarian, guarded liberal and no-platforming) to agree on the parameters for speech (including if there need to be limitations on particular use of language), so all feel able to participate
- Agree and keep to time limits to activities, e.g., 10 minutes for initial planning
- Agree concrete outcomes, e.g., group blog, essay, discussion panel, approach a Parliamentary Select Committee or All-Party Parliamentary Group

During the discussion:

- Keep lines of communication open in order to continue conversations: e.g., learn to keep quiet when enraged, and re-engage once calm again

Outcome and learnings:
Participants:

- Become sensitised to binary debates (e.g., Israel/Palestine), thereby avoiding a refusal to consider compromise
- Develop a clear personal moral framework for conversation that can work for both individuals and groups
- Understand the importance of debating societal values and purposes
- Use evidence-based learning
- Use a range of approaches, e.g., philosophy, sociology or religion in the search for meaning
- Become prepared to discuss common contestable concepts: e.g., *Fundamental British Values*
- Frequently discuss ethical reasoning in groups
- Understand others' perspectives and different points of view

How it is chaired:
There are trained facilitator(s) who explain that their role is not to lead, but to ensure the group develops its own parameters and to make sure each group member follows them. Most universities train students in consent training, mediation and conflict resolution work, and these packages can be adapted for the more educational purposes of the CofI.

Appendix: Community of Inquiry (CofI)

1. The facilitator explains that there will be group work that will lead to an outcome
2. Without intervention from the facilitator, participants choose one stimulus from several options that are of interest
3. The facilitator makes it clear that this topic is controversial and may show up differences within the group that were hitherto unseen
4. Participants are prepared for a discussion, ask questions and follow agreed-upon rules
5. The facilitator participates little in the discussion except to ensure ground rules are followed, and an outcome is achieved

Procedural values are central to the CofI. These include values to which we may already subscribe, but they should be discussed explicitly at the start of the process:

- A sense of community
- Inquiry-based learning
- Respect for others
- Using evidence to back up assertions
- Active listening
- Turn-taking to help facilitate participation from groups that are sometimes marginalised in debate, such as women from ethnic minority backgrounds
- Arguing for the opposite side
- Tolerance of different viewpoints and a commitment to pluralism
- Acceptance of, but also a challenge to, the ideology of difference
- Acceptance of shared risk of causing offence and the need to mitigate it reciprocally
- Humility, including a willingness to acknowledge the limits of one's knowledge
- Hopefulness that open discussion can lead to positive change
- Acceptance that the outcome may be agreeing to differ

Example from experience

Scott-Baumann created a CofI as the final session of a first-year undergraduate module on Islam, within a Religion, Philosophy and Ethics degree (Scott-Baumann 2010).

The students met two devout British Muslim scholars and discussed Islam and terrorism with them. All the students were white, described themselves as secular and most said they were sceptical about Islam and worried about terrorism.

Scott-Baumann used this model because over time, she observed that undergraduates came to the module on Islam with interest and also with many strong preconceptions about Muslims (having the propensity to be radicalised for terrorism, oppressing women and keeping themselves isolated from British society). She wanted the students to meet Muslim scholars in an atmosphere of trust and as a group have an open dialogue about Islam.

At the outset of the discussion, all present established the ground rules and parameters for discussion. Scott-Baumann urged the students to speak as freely as possible and to express their opinions without fear of causing offence, noting the importance of this for the learning process and that the scholars supported the approach. This helped the students become comfortable with expressing their true opinions. Thus she established the liberal approach as the default position for the conversation. At times, the conversation bordered on the libertarian approach, when some students made comments using language that others found offensive. Scott-Baumann encouraged the students to discuss why these terms might be considered offensive. In order to continue the conversation in a way where all felt comfortable, it was agreed that these terms should not be used for the remainder of the session; thus the discussion returned to the liberal approach.

Because the liberal approach assumes that matters regarding ethnicity, race and religion can be discussed freely, the students asked impertinent questions. Yet by this process they came to acknowledge there is a contradiction between viewing Islam as a risk versus upholding the principle of respecting religions, enshrined in the Equality Act 2010 and the Human Rights Act 1998. The Muslim scholars reported afterwards that they sometimes found the students rude, but for the sake of the discussion they held back their criticism of the students' views; thus the scholars deployed a guarded liberal approach to speech. The guarded liberal approach assumes that matters regarding ethnicity, race and religion will touch on sensitivities inherent to the topic, and that open discussion must be carefully and respectfully negotiated, following Kamali (1997). The scholars had undertaken their own informal risk assessment before agreeing to attend and felt they were risk-aware enough to make the encounter worth undertaking for the sake of establishing some sort of reciprocity.

This was a one-off. Such work only becomes truly productive over time with several sessions. Regular discussions could follow that would involve more negotiations about limits, while also establishing more parity of esteem within the group.

By the end of the session, the students came to understand the scholars' viewpoints. They identified the session as a highpoint of the module and gained increased awareness of key issues through the scholars' answers:

- Terrorism ('Islam is against this violence, and the Qur'an tells us to obey the laws of the land we live in')
- Choice in religious practice and dress ('I dress like this because it reminds me that I am a believer, not because I am forced')
- Interfaith links ('we work with Jews and Christians')
- Education ('we teach a wide range of GCSEs at our college and five A Level options, including sociology and psychology')
- Foreign policy ('we would welcome more open debate in the UK; this is our country too').

References

Chwalisz, C. (2019) 'A New Wave of Deliberative Democracy', *Carnegie Europe*, 26 November. https://carnegieeurope.eu/2019/11/26/new-wave-of-deliberative-democracy-pub-80422.

Hankinson Nelson, L. (1993) 'Epistemological Communities'. In Alcoff, L, and Potter, E. (eds.) *Feminist Epistemologies*. New York: Routledge: 121–159.

Kamali, M.H. (1997) *Freedom of Expression in Islam*. Cambridge: Islamic Texts Society.

Lee, Y. and Rofe, J.S. (2016) 'Paragogy and Flipped Assessment: Experience of Designing and Running a MOOC on Research Methods', *Open Learning: The Journal of Open, Distance and e-Learning*, 31, 2: 116–129. http://dx.doi.org/10.1080/02680513.2016.1188690.

Reiff, B. (2019) 'Can the Israel-Palestine Campus War Become a Conversation?', *Haaretz*, 21 July. https://www.haaretz.com/world-news/.premium-can-the-israel-palestine-campus-war-become-a-conversation-1.7545514.

Salmon, G. (2013) *E-tivities: The Key to Active Online Learning*. 2nd ed. London and New York: Routledge.

Scott-Baumann, A. (2010) 'A Community of Inquiry: Talking to Muslims'. In Farrar, M. (ed.) *The Study of Islam within Social Science Curricula in UK Universities: Case Studies 1*. Centre for Sociology, Anthropology and Politics, Higher Education Academy: 81–84. https://www.heacademy.ac.uk/system/files/max_farrar_case_studies.pdf.

Index

Page numbers in *italic* indicate figures. Page numbers in **bold** indicate tables.

Abou El Fadl, K. 15, 28, 30, 44, 56, 102
Agamben, G. 34
agonism 35, 44
Al Baghal, T. 105
All-Party Parliamentary Group (APPG) 129, 134
anti-Semitism 108, 119
Arabic 72
Arts and Humanities Research Council (AHRC) 9, 70, 77–81, 104–105
autonomy 16–19, 24, 28, 63, 74, 108

Barendt, E. 18–19
Beard, M. 4, 12, 120, 124
Begg, Moazzam 96
blasphemy 14; Prophet Muhammad cartoons 39
Boycott, Divestment, Sanctions (BDS) 94, 104
Butler, J. 20, 23, 26, 37, 83, 125
bullshit 36, 38
Butt, Salman 52–53, 122, 129

CAGE 68, 96, 100, 104, 115, 116, 117
campaign 40, 46, 73, 84, 85, 89, 90, 92–94, 98, 99, 103, 104, 117, 119, 123
categorical imperative 17, 58, 114, 117; *see also* Kant, E.
Catholic 13, 28, 117
censorship 29, 38, 41, 125, 130
Charity Commission 3, 5, 9, 84, 88–118, 120, 122–123, 129, 131; concern about extremism 102–104, 108–115; students' knowledge of 104–106
charity law 88–92; *see also* public benefit requirement
chilling effect 3, 61, 80, 83, 98, 103
Christianity 61, 65, 84
Chwalisz, C. 8, 10, 35, 44, 61, 45, 121, 124, 131, 133, 137
citizenship 11, 24, 47, 61, 68, 79, 116, 132
community 13, 14, 18, 23, 42, 44, 49, 69, 76
Community of Inquiry 8, 9, 24, 30, 38, 79, 120, 123, 130, 132–137
conflict resolution 79, 124, 134
consequences 5, 16, 28, 61, 79, 98, 111
consequentialist 16, 17, 19, 24
conservative 73, 76, 97; social 1, 7, 9, 40, 72, 73, 76, 83, 84, 94, 97–98, 100, 103, 120
Conservative 1, 40, 71, 94, 103; *see also* neoconservative
CONTEST 48, 50, 51
conversation 119–137
counter-terrorism 1, 7, 48–52, 54, 58, 62, 70, 81–82
Counter-Terrorism and Security Act (CTSA) 1, 48, 50–52

decisionism 34, 35, 63
democracy 2, 3, 13, 15, 17, 18, 24, 34, 37, 46, 47, 50, 95, 111, 133; deficit of 7, 22, 83, 102, 105, 121; deliberative 33, 35, 45, 99, 115, 121, 123–124, 130–131, 137;

Index 139

liberal 1, 6, 21, 32–33, 41, 44, 119, 128, 130
Department of Communities and Local Government (DCLG) 49
depoliticisation 95, 123
dignity 6, 13, 19, 78
Dworkin, R. 18, 21, 28

Education (No. 2) Act 1986 52, 91
Education Act 1994 89
elite: liberal as 44, 119; students as 82, 119; *see also* people v elite
Emwazi, Mohammed 103
Equality and Human Rights Commission (EHRC) 5, 112, 122
Europe 13, 15, 17, 32, 33, 35–36, 71, 103
European Union 33, 36
exempt charity status 89, 98, 106
external speakers 2, 28, 43, 48, 51, 52, 55, 61, 96–97, 104, 107–112, 128; vetting 53, 97, 108–110, 125
extreme speech 12, 19, 23, 111
extremism 1, 4–5, 15, 49–54, 57–59, 62–63, 70–73, 80, 96, 127; definitions of 91, 107–108, 111; extent in universities 1, 55–56; *see also* Charity Commission; external speakers; Henry Jackson Society (HJS)
Extremism Risk Guidance (ERG) 54

Farage, Nigel 36, 40, 42, 71, 75
feminism/t 20, 21, 26, 43, 80, 96, 133
Fish, S. 21–23, 88, 90, 93–94, 98
freedom of speech: default university position 26, 41, 53, 92, 113–114, 121, 123, 128, 136; fourfold model of 9, 12, 24, 27, 123–124, 127–128, 134; government intervention into 1–2, 51–53, 102–115, 119; populist appeals to 32–47; university policies 48–87, 97
Fundamental British Values 50, 52, 72, 78, 111, 134

gender 20, 35, 78, 120, 124; *see also* transgender
Green, A. 36–37

guarded liberal approach to freedom of speech 3, 19–21, 25–27, 40–41, 51, 53, 58, 63, 73–74, 76, 78, 82, 93, 96, 98, 114, 121, 125–126, 134, 136
Guest, M. 59, 72, 77–82, 120

Habermas, J. 23–24, 26, 36, 125
Hadith 14, 15, 72
Hankinson Nelson, L. 23, 83, 123, 133
harm 3–4, 13, 16–20, 26, 32, 51, 54, 76, 91, 102, 107, 125; Mill's harm principle 17, 19; Ricoeur on 99
hate speech 4–5, 18–20, 23, 25, 32, 40–42, 51, 63, 77, 83, 114, 129; bans on 18, 23; online 4, 35–36
Heath-Kelly, C. 49–51, 62
Henry Jackson Society (HJS) 9, 52, 55, 70, 103, 128; *see also* Student Rights
hijab 58, 78
Hillman, N. 75, 83
Home Office 48–62, 71, 109, 111, 122

ideology 33, 42, 51, 54, 123, 135
immigration 71, 103
interfaith 79, 85, 127, 137
ISIS 3, 51, 55, 93
Islam 4, 9, 12, 13–15, 44, 39, 49, 51–57, 62, 64, 71–72, 78–83, 103–107, 135–137; *see also* Re/presenting Islam on Campus
Islamic law 13–15, 71–72, 111
Islamic Societies (ISoc) 107–114, 121, 127
Islamism 44, 49, 54–9, 71, 107
Islamophobia 32, 38–40, 53–54, 64, 71, 77–79, 120, 129
Israel 43, 76, 83, 94–95, 104, 108–109, 113, 134

Jewish people 15, 16, 43, 76, 80, 95, 109, 133, 137
jihad 3, 51, 55, 72, 103
Jihadi John *see* Emwazi, Mohammed

Index

Joint Committee on Human Rights (JCHR) 2, 52, 90, 97, 102, 122, 129
Johnson, Boris 35, 38, 40
Joseph Rowntree Charitable Trust (JCRT) 103–104

Kamali, M.H. 15, 136
Kant, E. 16–18, 23, 25, 48, 58, 102, 108, 114; *see also* categorical imperative

Laclau, E. 34–38, 44
left-wing 1, 34, 40, 43, 62
liberal approach to freedom of speech 16, 18–19, 21–27, 32–47, 70–87, 96, 124–125, 128, 134, 136
libertarian approach to freedom of speech 3, 6, 9, 17–19, 21–22, 25, 32, 39–43, 70, 73, 75–76, 78, 82, 119, 125–126, 134, 136
lying 16, 17, 37, 108

media 38, 39, 41, 43, 70, 74, 77, 79, 97, 103, 107, 109, 112–115, 120, 122, 124, 128–130
Mill, J.S. 17–20, 23, 25–26, 83
minority 1, 4, 6, 37–38, 41–42, 56, 72, 74, 76–79, 82–83, 95–96, 115, 120, 124, 135
moral 40–41, 44, 48, 119, 126, 134
moral panic 2, 6, 40–41, 44, 70, 74–75, 82, 115, 119, 128
Mosques and Imams National Advisory Board (MINAB) 49
Mouffe, C. 34–36, 44, 124
Müller, J. 34, 37
Myerson, M. 36

National Audit Office (NAO) 102–103
National Union of Students (NUS) 42, 76, 78, 95
neoconservative 7, 9, 52, 70, 71
no-platforming approach to freedom of speech 2–3, 7, 19–20, 22–23, 26, 33, 40–43, 51, 53, 58, 63, 70, 75–76, 82, 92–93, 96, 98, 111, 113–114, 119–121, 126, 134

Obama, Barack 37
Office for Students (OfS) 2, 55, 61, 64, 63, 72, 98, 120
online 4, 8, 32, 36, 49, 51, 57, 70, 72–3, 79, 109, 133

Palestine 43, 76, 94–95, 108–114, 127, 134
Palestine Society 108–114
pedagogy 24, 55, 83, 123–124
Peirce, C.S. 8, 23–24, 124, 133
people v elite 33, 37–38; *see also* elite
Perfect, S. 1, 4, 40, 72, 75–76, 79, 81, 127, 129
persuasion principle, Strauss's 17, 48, 63, 108
Plato 12
police 7, 50, 123
populism 32–47, 129; left-wing 43; right-wing 32–34, 37, 38, 43, 44, 112
Pragmatism 8, 22, 24, 124
Prevent 1, 3, 5, 9, 48–69, 70–87; criticisms of 49–50, 53–58; development of 49–53; Duty Guidance 48, 52–53, 63, 107, 109, 122; Leads in universities 48–68; and Muslims 48–69; training materials 57–58, 60, 122
procedural values 124, 135
public benefit requirement 91, 108, 111

Qur'an 15, 137
Qurashi, F. 54, 56, 59

Rabb, I. 14
racism 4, 18, 22, 26, 75, 78
radicalisation 4–5, 49, 51, 54–60, 62–63, 70, 80–81, 107–108, 119–120, 122, 128; in universities 55–56
reciprocity 5, 8, 21, 24, 26, 115, 1126–127, 136
Reiff, B. 95, 133

Index

religion 12, 14–16, 24, 38, 71–72, 78, 80, 97, 105, 134–136
religious reasoning 23, 125, 127
Re/presenting Islam on Campus 9, 39, 42, 70, 77–83, 104, 120
rhetoric 32, 35–38, 43, 52
Ricoeur, P. 8, 21, 30, 33, 37, 88, 99, 126
rights 6–8, 14, 16, 18, 21, 25–26, 32–47, 63, 74, 119, 120, 125; animal 107; Bentham, J. 6; human rights 6–8, 13, 32–47, 52; Human Rights Act 1998 5, 136
right-wing *see* populism
risk 5–6, 12, 14, 20, 34–35, 38, 52, 53, 59–60, 62, 135–136; assessment 93, 104, 108–110, 136; aversion 3, 7–9, 19, 26, 28, 43–44, 53, 58–59, 63–64, 81, 83, 92, 98, 113–114, 120–121, 130; awareness 7–8, 124, 136; *see also* Extremism Risk Guidance

sabbatical officers 88, 92–96, 99
safeguarding 57–60
safe space 2, 41, 61, 76–77, 96
Scott-Baumann, A. 24, 33, 37, 42, 52, 55, 70, 72, 80, 109–110, 120, 124, 129–130, 135–136
Schmitt, C. 34, 38, 48, 63; *see also* decisionism
secularism 13, 15, 23, 26, 39, 111, 125, 127, 136
securitisation 111, 122
select committee 129, 134
shari'a *see* Islamic law
Shawcross, William 103–104, 112
Skinner, B. 54–55
Slater, A. 15, 56, 73–74, 111
snowflakes 40, 74, 119
social media 4, 35–36, 93, 107, 109, 130
Socrates 12, 26

Sorial, S. 20, 23, 26, 73, 82, 102, 111, 114
Spiked 9, 70, 73–75, 77, 82–83, 128
Spinoza, B. 15–16, 18, 25
Spinwatch 71
Strauss, D. 17, 25, 48, 63, 108, 125; *see also* persuasion principle
Student Rights 52, 70–71; *see also* Henry Jackson Society (HJS)
students' unions 3, 5, 9, 10, 41–42, 53, 63, 74, 84, 88–99, 102–115, 119, 120–123, 128–130; Chief Executive Officers (CEOs) of 88, 92–99, 102, 106–108; governance of 89, 97–98, 102–115

terrorism 1, 3, 10, 19, 49–53, 56–57, 60–63, 71–72, 81, 91, 104, 120, 135–137; Terrorism Act 2000 49; *see also* counter-terrorism and Counter-Terrorism and Security Act 2015
Theos 75, 81, 127
tolerance 50, 75, 82, 124, 135
transgender 43
trust 36, 58, 62, 83, 124, 126–127, 136
trustee 91, 93–95, 98–99, 106–110, 112, 122, 123
truth 16–19, 24, 26, 36, 44, 60, 111, 129

utilitarian 6, 16
utopia 42, 44, 123

values *see* Fundamental British Values
violence 4, 7–8, 15, 18, 49, 58–59, 77, 91, 137

Waldron, J. 19–20, 25–26, 41, 51, 73, 114
women 12, 40, 49, 58, 78–79, 82, 120, 124, 135–136

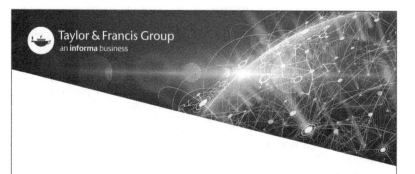